©HEAP PROTECTION: COPYRIGHT HANDBOOK for FILMS

Entertainment Industry Series, Volume I
2nd Edition

**Step-by-Step Guide
To Copyright Your Film
Without a Lawyer**

M. M. Le Blanc, JD, MBA

Veteran Hollywood Studio Executive * Entertainment Attorney * Educator

BOOKS by M. M. Le BLANC

Award-winning Entertainment Business

CHEAP PROTECTION: COPYRIGHT HANDBOOK for FILMS
CHEAP PROTECTION: COPYRIGHT HANDBOOK for SCREENPLAYS
CHEAP PROTECTION: COPYRIGHT HANDBOOK for TELEPLAYS
CHEAP PROTECTION: COPYRIGHT HANDBOOK for TV PROJECTS
CHEAP PROTECTION: COPYRIGHT HANDBOOK for MUSIC
FINANCING INDEPENDENT FILMS: 50 WAYS TO GET THE GOLDEN GOOSE, NOT A GOOSE EGG
FILM EQUITY CROWDFUNDING: 10 LEGAL WAYS TO SELL EQUITY IN YOUR FILM

Award-Winning Fiction

EVANGELINE: PARADISE STOLEN, Volumes I and II, True 1st Edition
EVANGELINE: PARADISE STOLEN, Volumes I and II, Ltd. 2nd Edition
EVANGELINE: PARADISE STOLEN, Volume III
EVANGELINE: PARADISE STOLEN, Volume I, 3rd edition
EVANGELINE: PARADISE STOLEN, Volume II, 3rd edition
EVANGELINE: PARADISE STOLEN, Volumes I and II, 3rd edition
THE PITCHER'S PRAYER, A Novel about Faith, Family, the First Amendment...and Baseball

Award-Winning Non-Fiction

ACADIE THEN AND NOW, Collective Work, Author, "Acadians in Belle Île en Mer, France"
L'ACADIE HIER ET AUJOURD'HUI, Collective Work, Editor, "Les Acadiens de Belle Île en Mer"
THE ACADIAN MIRACLE, 50th Anniversary Edition
THE ACADIAN MIRACLE, 53rd Anniversary Edition with Index
THE TRUE STORY OF THE ACADIANS, 90th Anniversary Edition
THE TRUE STORY OF THE ACADIANS, 93rd Anniversary Edition with Index

ENTERTAINMENT BUSINESS BOOKS
Published by

ENTERTAINMENT INDUSTRY SERIES

COPYRIGHT

VOL. 1, CHEAP PROTECTION: COPYRIGHT HANDBOOK for FILMS
VOL. 2, CHEAP PROTECTION: COPYRIGHT HANDBOOK for SCREENPLAYS
VOL. 3, CHEAP PROTECTION: COPYRIGHT HANDBOOK for TELEPLAYS
VOL. 4, CHEAP PROTECTION: COPYRIGHT HANDBOOK for TV PROJECTS
VOL. 5, CHEAP PROTECTION: COPYRIGHT HANDBOOK for MUSIC
VOL. 6, CHEAP PROTECTION: COPYRIGHT HANDBOOK FOR LITERARY WORKS

FILM FINANCING

VOL. 1, FINANCING INDEPENDENT FILMS: 50 WAYS TO GET THE GOLDEN GOOSE, NOT A GOOSE EGG
VOL. 2, FILM EQUITY CROWDFUNDING: 10 LEGAL WAYS TO SELL EQUITY IN YOUR FILM

*For my former film school students,
may you aspire to even greater heights of success
in building wealth in the entertainment industry
through your Intellectual Property*

*PARIS N'EST PAS FAIT EN UN JOUR !
Merci St. Gabriel*

©HEAP PROTECTION:
COPYRIGHT HANDBOOK for FILMS
Entertainment Industry Series, Volume 1
2nd Edition
by M.M. Le Blanc

Step-by-Step Guide
To Copyright Your Film
Without a Lawyer

©2016, 2021 BizEntine Press
All rights reserved.

Print ISBN: 978-1-947471-18-4
epub ISBN: 978-1-947471-15-3
mobi ISBN: 978-1-947471-36-8

No part of this book may be copied, duplicated, translated, reproduced, disseminated, transmitted, stored, archived, retrieved, or otherwise used in any manner and in any media now known or hereafter devised without the publisher's prior written authorization.

Cover Design: BizEntine Press
Cover Design ©2016, 2021 BizEntine Press

Manufactured in the United States of America by

CONTENTS

BOOKS BY M. M. Le BLANC	**3**
BIZENTINE PRESS ENTERTAINMENT BUSINESS BOOKS	**4**
INTRODUCTION	**9**

PART ONE: YOUR ADVENTURES IN WONDERLAND
Discovering Copyright — **11**
1. OVERVIEW: What You Will Learn in This Book — 13
2. WHAT: What Copyright Is and How It Works — 20
3. WHO: Who Can Copyright & Own a Film — 37
4. WHY: Why History & Law Create a Powerful Asset — 48

PART TWO: CAN YOU HANDLE THE TRUTH ABOUT COPYRIGHT?
Everything You Always Wanted to Know About It but Didn't Want to Hire a Lawyer to Do — **55**
5. EXCLUSIVE RIGHTS: The "Bundle of Rights" Builds Wealth — 57
6. INFRINGEMENT: What About Unauthorized Use — 73
7. DURATION: How Long Copyrights Last — 97

PART THREE: BE YOUR OWN WOLF OF WALL STREET
Add Film Value Without Increasing the Budget — **103**
8. FAIR USE: Using Copyrighted Work (Legally) — 105
9. PUBLIC DOMAIN: Free Public Domain Content vs. Free or Fee-Based Licensed Content — 112
10. DESIGN ASSETS: Film-Related Designs vs. VARA Works — 119

PART FOUR: DIGITAL WAR OF THE WORLDS
The Copyright Digital Age & Beyond — **125**
11. DMCA: The Long Arm of the Law Against Digital Piracy — 127

PART FIVE: IT'S A SMALL, SMALL, SMALL, SMALL WORLD
International Copyright Agreements, Issues & Solutions — **135**

12. INTERNATIONAL RIGHTS: Protect Your Copyright Globally
    Without Leaving Home 137

PART SIX: THERE'S NO CRYING IN COPYRIGHTS! Step-by-Step Registration to DIY Right Every Time 145

13. REGISTRATION: Step-by-Step Guide to Copyright Your
    Film Without a Lawyer 147
14. RESEARCH: Search for Copyrights Online or In-Person 164
15. PRIVACY & PUBLICITY RIGHTS: The Effect on Film Content ... 172
16. BUSINESS ENTITIES: The Right Legal Structure for Your Film
    and Your Business 176
17. 2021 LEGISLATIVE UPDATE: Small Claims 182
18. CONCLUSION: That's a Wrap! 184

TABLES
Table 2-A: Copyright Notice, Published Work 34
Table 2-B: Copyright Notice, Unpublished Work 36
Table 6-A: Infringement, Actual Damages 81
Table 6-B: Infringement, Statutory Damages 82
Table 6-C: Comparison Actual vs. Statutory Damages 84
Table 7-A: Duration 102
Table 13-A: Step-by-Step eCO Copyright Registration - Film ... 152
Table FB-A: Instructions to Complete Form PA 188
Table FB-B: Instructions to Complete Form VA 189

FORMS BANK 185
REFERENCES 192
FIAPF - INTL FEDERATION OF FILM PRODUCERS ASSOC. 195
FREE & ALMOST FREE MATERIALS 196
INDEX 201
CONTACT THE PUBLISHER, CONTACT THE AUTHOR ... 208
ABOUT THE AUTHOR 208

INTRODUCTION

This *Copyright Handbook for Films* is different from any other book about copyrights because it is written specifically for you: -non-lawyer filmmakers, producers, directors, film students, educators and others.

What is the first thing you think of when you hear the word "copyright"? If you are like most people in the entertainment industry, it is a foreign language, "legalese." Not this book. With a step-by-step guide in plain English, you learn to copyright your film without a lawyer or legal jargon. But this book is also a valuable forms library, a resource and research collection, a hands-on course in copyrights for students and a refresher course for industry professionals and educators.

Keep this useful tool as a desk reference, production office guide and textbook answering common questions and issues related to creating, protecting and defending your film rights, and your film-related designs that can also be copyrighted.

This *Copyright Handbook for Films* provides general information but is not legal advice, nor is it to be used as a substitute for personal legal advice from a qualified attorney on any specific issues and questions.

ORGANIZATION OF BOOK

The book is organized in concise, easy-to-read Chapters, which are grouped into six Parts by theme. Each Part builds and strengthens your foundation of knowledge about copyright to give you a better understanding of it, specifically relating to films, film design assets and the entertainment industry. Each Chapter focuses on a major subject about copyright, with detailed sub-topics and graphic Tables.

BUILD WEALTH IN THE ENTERTAINMENT INDUSTRY

THE BASIS OF ALL WEALTH IN THE ENTERTAINMENT INDUSTRY IS INTELLECTUAL PROPERTY. This book shows you how to build wealth in the entertainment industry by protecting your intellectual property., particularly the five exclusive rights of copyright -- the rights to copy, distribute, display, perform, or adapt into derivative creative works -- which filmmakers can exploit to generate revenues and profits. You will also receive valuable step-by-step guides for copyright registration to protect films and other assets you may not know can be copyrighted.

ANSWERS TO COMMON FILMMAKER QUESTIONS

- How can I copyright a film without paying a lawyer?
- How can I legally use someone else's work free?
- What can I do about unauthorized online uploads of my films?
- Can I copyright designs created for the film?
- Does the "poor man's copyright" provide legal protection?
- What is a work-for-hire agreement and how does it help me?
- If I sue an infringer and win, what could I receive in damages?

VALUABLE LESSONS YOU WISH YOU HAD KNOWN

- How to register a do-it-yourself copyright without a lawyer.
- How to build wealth as a filmmaker by copyrighting your creative works and exploiting the exclusive rights of copyright.
- How to access free content through public domain and fair use.
- How to protect your work from unauthorized use.
- How to resolve infringement without going to court.
- How to protect your work in countries around the world without ever leaving the United States.

BONUS FEATURES

- Forms Bank of Sample Filled-In Forms for Films & Storyboards
- 5 Exclusive Automatic Copyright Rights Owned by Filmmakers
- 9 Ways to Resolve Infringement Without Litigation
- 36 Producer Associations in 30 Countries
- 200+ Useful Contacts, Publications & References

Read, re-read and refer to this book over and over again, as you build your wealth in the entertainment industry. *Happy copyrighting!*

PART ONE

*

Your Adventures in Wonderland
Discovering Copyright

1. OVERVIEW

What You Will Learn in This Book

The basis of all wealth in the entertainment industry is intellectual property, often referred to as "IP." Filmmakers have an exciting opportunity, particularly in this digital age, to create original intellectual property works of authorship, adapt public domain and other free content into new works, and maximize their exploitation for profit.

The entertainment industry incorporates numerous creative arts categories in which IP is created, such as motion pictures, television, music, games, animation, and writing. Copyrightable creative works in these sectors include films, "making of" and "behind the scenes" films or videos, music videos, corporate or training films, television series, pilots, made-for-television movies and web series, as well as music, lyrics, scores, animated films or series, video games and distinctive characters in these creative works. Copyrightable material adapted for films, television productions and other works include screenplays, teleplays, pilots, outlines, synopses, treatments and bibles, as well as books, newspaper articles, blogs and much more.

In addition to IP in the works above, film-related artistic works also produce copyrightable works such as storyboard design, film poster design and art, still photography, production art and design, prop design and manufacture, costume design, prosthetics, choreography, and even tattoo design. The copyright rights in such works generates added value for the owners of such works.

Often, films and film-related designs involve multiple revisions and modifications prior to completing the finished product. Each version and revision constitutes a separate creative work in which copyright may be secured. For instance, an original screenplay or a script adapted from a book undergoes multiple revisions, rewrites and polishes. Films undergo multiple edits, rough cuts, and even final cuts by directors, studios, producers and more. Props, prosthetics, and masks are reworked until they are acceptable. Each work is copyrightable IP.

CHEAP PROTECTION: *Copyright Handbook for Films* is a valuable handbook, desk reference, textbook and refresher course rolled into one book. This book was written *specifically for non-lawyers* in the entertainment industry and in schools and colleges with film programs by an experienced industry insider, entertainment attorney, professor and academic Dean of entertainment law and business.

As Volume I in the *Entertainment Industry Series*, this book is an indispensable resource for filmmakers, producers, directors, educators, film students and anyone interested in protecting their IP. You will learn solutions to questions about copyrights for filmmakers, such as:

- What is copyright and how does it protect my film?
- How do I file a copyright registration without a lawyer?
- How can I copyright other elements created for my film?
- How could I legally use someone else's work free?
- What can I do if someone uploads or copies my film without my permission?
- How do I register my film with the U.S. Copyright Office?
- How can I do online copyright research?
- Does a celebrity's right to privacy or right to publicity prevent me from using content about him in my film?

This *Copyright Handbook for Film*s focuses on the who, what, why and how of copyright registration of films. Written in clear, concise language *without legalese* for ease of understanding, it serves as a valuable guide, textbook, reference and "how-to" desk manual.

This book also provides definitions, descriptions and step-by-step instructions for copyrighting a film. Note that use of the terms "film," "motion picture" or "movie" in this book refers collectively to a variety of creative audiovisual works, such as feature motion pictures, music videos, corporate videos, training videos, workout videos, film clips, and "making of" and "behind the scenes" promotional films., among others.

Other Volumes of this Series are individual *Copyright Handbooks* for other specific works of authorship created and exploited in the entertainment industry, including screenplays, music, teleplays and television projects and productions such as pilots, made-for-television movies, television series, and web series. Each Volume discusses and explains in non-legalese the ins and outs of copyrighting these original works of authorship in the entertainment industry.

Within the informative Chapters of this book, you will find easy-to-read material about copyrights for films in plain English, not in complex legal jargon. While copyright does involve legal issues such as infringement, federal and state laws, international treaties, and other topics the information is presented in an understandable way.

Information is presented on how to identify and copyright elements created for or used in a film that are IP assets available to generate additional revenues. Most filmmakers are unaware such film-related assets can be copyrighted independently of the audiovisual work, like:

- Storyboards,
- Unique on-set art,
- One-of-a-kind props,
- Hand-crafted masks,
- Original prosthetics,
- Unique hair or makeup designs,
- Original tattooes,
- On-set photographs, and
- Movie posters and the designs within them.

The material in this book is relevant to what you do as filmmakers, producers, directors, educators, film students and others interested in learning more about copyrighting works of authorship. Each of you will gain significant knowledge about the truths, myths, and "how-to" of copyrighting a film and its design elements.

Each Chapter begins with an overview of the concepts covered therein. Definitions, descriptions, examples, charts and resources are also provided for greater understanding.

In today's fast-paced digital world, information flows more freely than ever before. Ideas are exchanged on multiple devices and through multiple outlets such as online channels, streaming, links, social media posts, electronic mails and websites, as well as traditional communication forms like television, radio, print, outdoor and mail.

If all of this information is found in cyberspace, on television, on radio or in print, or in any of the myriad of ways in which ideas can be expressed shared and pirated, then the first question many ask is why bother with copyright? And the second question is how can films and other works be protected with this information flow, particularly online, throughout the world?

The main purpose of this *Copyright Handbook for Films* is to answer these questions from your perspective. You -- filmmakers, producers, directors, educators, film students and many others -- can gain valuable benefits through this book's discussions and explanations of copyright concepts. You will learn to identify, register and protect copyrightable assets and exploit them to build wealth in the entertainment industry. You are referred to as "filmmakers" going forward in this book.

SUMMARY OF SIX PARTS & EIGHTEEN CHAPTERS

This *Copyright Handbook for Films* is divided into six Parts, dividing the main subject matter into themes. Tables in certain Chapters provide additional graphic explanation for the copyright concepts and examples provided.

PART ONE. Chapters 1 through 4 provide copyright fundamentals. This Chapter 1 gives an overview of the book and the subject matter. Chapter 2 defines copyright and how it works, provides the criteria for a copyright and defines the types of works that qualify for copyright. This Chapter also explains how to give notice to the public of a valid copyright. Chapter 3 explains who qualifies as a copyright author or as an owner, when they are the same and when they are not. This Chapter discusses also the importance of the types of names that can be used to register a film for copyright, including actual legal names, pseudonyms, company names, and even anonymously, without any name. Chapter 4 discusses why copyright is a powerful asset to filmmakers with a concise explanation of the history of copyright law and important copyright legislation and international IP agreements.

PART TWO. Chapters 5, 6 and 7 explain the benefits, requirements and unauthorized use of copyrights. Chapter 5 discusses the various exclusive rights of a copyright owner in the "bundle of rights" and various means to exploit and profit from these exclusive rights. Chapter 6 explains infringement, the unauthorized use of a copyrighted work, and offers solutions and resolution tools for filmmakers to protect their work. Chapter 7 explains the duration, or period of time that copyrights are valid, and the different terms according to ownership or type of work.

PART THREE. Chapters 8, 9 and 10 inform how to exploit copyrights to increase a filmmaker's wealth and enhance the value of a film without increasing the budget. Chapter 8 explores the concept of "fair use" and how to use work copyrighted by third parties legally as well as how to obtain authorization to use a third party's work. Chapter 9 provides information on the "public domain" of free works and valuable resources providing free content for a filmmaker. Chapter 10 discusses how to protect copyright in film-related designs and summarizes key points of the Visual Artists Rights Act ("VARA").

PART FOUR. Chapter 11 discusses copyrights in the digital age of the internet and beyond, exploring the Digital Millennium Copyright Act and measures to protect digital works, including films. This Chapter also discusses issues related to digital piracy, illegal online peer-to-peer sharing and how to issue legal "take down" notices to remove unauthorized film uploads and postings from sites.

PART FIVE. Chapter 12 provides information on international copyright agreements, issues and solutions. This Chapter discusses the concept of international copyright protection through international treaties and trade agreements signed by the United States with foreign nations and how to protect a U.S. copyrighted film around the world in those nations without leaving the USA.

PART SIX. Chapters 13, 14, 15, 16, 17 and 18 offer filmmakers tools to register and protect their films, as well as other valuable information. Chapter 13 provides step-by-step instructions how to open a free account on the U.S. Copyright Office ("USCO") Electronic Copyright registration site, eCO, and a step-by-step guide to register your film for copyright electronically and using paper forms. Chapter 14 offers step-by-step directions to performing copyright research online and how to obtain other research from the USCO. Chapter 15 discusses the right of privacy and the right of publicity, which may affect the use of content in a film. Chapter 16 explains numerous business structures that can be used by filmmakers to create a production company, a Special Purpose Entity for a film and a sole proprietorship with a fictitious business name, as well as how a filmmaker protects himself from liability. Chapter 17 gives a legislative update on a new Copyright Claims Board. The final Chapter 18 provides a summary of this *Copyright Handbook for Films* with final words about building wealth in the industry through IP.

BONUS MATERIALS

This *Copyright Handbook for Films* also includes a substantial number of Bonus Materials in the back of the book offering additional valuable information, including the following:

- **INDEX.** A list of frequently used words and phrases in the book and the pages for easy reference.

- **FORMS BANK.** Sample filled-in copyright Form PA (Performing Arts/Motion Pictures) for a film and Form VA (Visual Arts) for a storyboard and step-by-step instructions for copyrighting works using these forms.

- **REFERENCES.** Over 200 useful contacts in the entertainment industry, film-related resources, with websites or other contact information for the U.S. Copyright Office, the U.S. Patent & Trademark Office, industry Guilds, associations and unions, entertainment trade publications, CMOs (Collective

Management Organizations), ADR (Alternative Dispute Resolution) administration organizations and other important contacts for filmmakers, producers, directors, music video producers, as well as educators and film students and all others involved in creating and owning films and other audiovisual works.

- **FIAPF - INTERNATIONAL FEDERATION OF FILM PRODUCERS ASSOCIATION.** A listing of 36 producer associations in 30 countries.

- **FREE MATERIALS & ALMOST FREE MATERIALS.** Materials including free Circulars published online by the U.S. Copyright Office to provide additional guidance and assistance to filmmakers. Websites for FEDFLIX and Public.Resource.Org are also provided, which give access to public domain U.S. government documents and films, sites for other sources of free and almost-free materials including Project Gutenberg and Creative Commons, as well as numerous sites for books, eBooks and other free or almost free licensed content. Much of this content is public domain or free for personal use, although use for commercial purposes may require a license.

2. WHAT

What Copyright Is & How It Works

This Chapter provides the definition of copyright, the elements required for a copyright and how copyright protects original works of authorship, including films, in the United States. Additionally, the point when copyright subsists, or is created and exists, in a film is discussed.

COPYRIGHT DEFINITION

To learn how to copyright and protect your film, you must first know the definition of copyright. Copyright is an exclusive legal right granted by law to creators of original works of authorship that are fixed in a tangible medium of expression.

To "fix" a work in a "tangible medium of expression" is to put a work of authorship in a physical form that can be perceived. For this reason, ideas cannot be copyrighted. However, the expression of the idea can be copyrighted once it is fixed in a tangible form. And, an expression that is virtually the only way to express an idea is not copyrightable.

In addition to ideas, copyright protection also does not extend to titles or procedures, mathematical formulas, methods of operation and other such concepts. Other forms of intellectual property including patents, trademarks and trade secrets may protect these works.

Many types of creative audiovisual works are covered by United States copyright law. Some of these include motion pictures, music videos, "making of" and "behind the scenes" films or videos, corporate and training films, workout videos, and screenplays, storyboards, art, music, sculptures, masks, designs, drawings, photographs and tattooes.

DROIT MORAL / MORAL RIGHTS

Copyright law in the United States protects the economic rights of authors of copyrighted works of authorship. In addition, authors of certain visual works of fine art are also granted non-economic interest "moral rights," in the Visual Artists Rights Act of 1990 ("VARA").

Moral rights stem from the French "droit moral" rights of authors to protect their honor and reputation through their works. Moral rights are prevalent in many civil law countries, such as France, that even preclude an author from waiving or transferring his moral rights to the buyer of the work. VARA is discussed in Chapter 10.

IDEA vs. EXPRESSION

As seen above, though ideas are not copyrightable, the expression of that idea in film, writing, music, poetry, art and other tangible forms is eligible for copyright protection. The expression must be fixed in any tangible medium that can be perceived or otherwise communicated directly or indirectly with the aid of a device or machine.

In examining whether a work is eligible for copyright, it must meet the two criteria below:
- The work must be an original work of authorship which includes at least some creative effort, and,
- The work must be fixed in a tangible medium of expression.

As stated earlier in this Chapter, in very limited circumstances the expression of an idea is not copyrightable. This is known as the "merger doctrine," where an idea and its expression are inseparable, making both unable to be protected by copyright. This theory provides that the idea and the expression of it merge when there are so few ways to express such an idea.

For instance, romantic comedies usually have a "boy meets girl, boy loses girl, boy gets girl" structure. That expression cannot be copyrighted because it would create, in essence, a monopoly precluding anyone else from expressing a rom-com in any other way.

SCÈNES À FAIRE

Another concept in filmmaking from France precluding copyright of certain work is, "scènes à faire," which literally means "scenes to do" or "scenes to make" (in a film). This concept provides that a scene in a film usually necessary for a particular genre or type of film cannot be copyrighted. For filmmakers, this includes elements that are practically required to be in such a film for it to fit into the genre, such as a generic type of character, story structure, scene and the like.

For example, every horror film needs a monster, so generic monsters are not copyrightable. However, expressing the monster as original and distinctive makes the work eligible for copyright.

ORIGINAL CREATIVE WORK OF AUTHORSHIP

To determine the first copyright requirement, decide how a work of authorship can be original and creative. The author must create an acceptable form of an original work alone or with other authors.

Although the additional requirement of creative effort was not included in the Copyright Clause or later legislation, creativity was determined by the United States Supreme Court in 1991. The case was *Feist Publications vs. Rural Telephone Service Co.*, 499 U.S. 340 (1991). The Court held that a white pages telephone directory of an alphabetical listing of names, addresses and numbers did not qualify for copyright because it lacked even a minimum of creative effort.

Since then, creativity is an important requirement for copyrighting works. After the *Feist* case, an original work of authorship must embody at least some creativity in order to be copyrighted. Though the law does not specify how much "creative effort" is required, the act of copying names and addresses does not meet that standard.

To understand more about creativity, consider a synopsis you have written for a romantic comedy film as, "Boy meets girl, boy loses girl, boy gets girl." In addition, you write a synopsis for a horror film as, "A monster with an ax terrorizes teenagers in a cabin in the woods." Unfortunately, neither expression fulfills the requirements of originality and creativity for copyright. The first is the generic structure of a rom-com. The second is a scène a faire of a horror film.

However, the specific expression of these commonplace ideas in romantic comedies and horror films can be copyrighted if they are original and creative. Suppose you re-write the following romantic comedy synopsis, which you entitle, "The Cellist" as follows.

"The King of an undersea realm hears the haunting music of a cellist on the beach. He falls in love with her but she accepts her boyfriend's marriage proposal. When the groom is a no-show at the church, the cellist returns to the beach playing music that is even more haunting. The King proposes and they wed and live happily ever after in his kingdom."

Now the story is original and creative even though it uses the generic structure of boy meets, loses and gets the girl.

The horror film idea can be rewritten with distinctive fictional characters and unique elements that are copyrightable, such as:

"A teenage alien lands near a cabin in a secluded wood where a group of high schoolers tell scary stories by a campfire. On the alien's planet, wielding an ax is a sign of friendship, but when he waves his ax at the teens they scream and run away, dropping their phones. He takes smiling selfies on the devices, leaving them outside the cabin. One teen, an art student, finally understands and convinces the others to befriend the alien, and everyone is sad when the alien returns to his planet."

With these details, the monster found in a horror genre film has been transformed into a unique expression of an idea about a monster. As a result, the story is copyrightable, and was copyrighted when fixed in the medium of the manuscript of this book. The next requirement for a work to be copyrightable is fixation in a tangible medium of expression. This concept is presented below.

FIXED IN A TANGIBLE MEDIUM OF EXPRESSION

The second requirement for a copyrightable work is that it be "fixed in a tangible medium of expression." This means putting the work into a physical form, a concrete media or another means to perceive the expression of your idea. The work may be fixed directly so that it can be seen or heard even after it was spoken, performed, filmed or recorded. Examples of direct fixation of a work include hand writing a director's notes onto a shooting script or drawing a storyboard.

Alternatively, the work may be fixed indirectly with the assistance of a device or machine like filming with a digital camera, recording sound or designing a storyboard with computer software. Merely thinking about a story idea for a film or mentioning it to someone is still just an idea that cannot be copyrighted. However, typing the expression into a device, saving it to a computer or writing it by hand fixes the expression of an idea in a tangible medium that can be perceived directly or indirectly.

Expressing a story idea for a film to your friend in an elevator is not fixed. That is just a spoken idea that could be overheard and used by anyone without any liability. You shared an idea orally, but that idea was not expressed in any tangible form. However, if you recorded your conversation while in the elevator, your idea would be an expression fixed in the tangible medium of a sound recording.

Rehearsals for a film that are not taped, videoed or otherwise recorded are not copyrightable works of authorship because they are not fixed in a tangible medium. No one can watch, or perceive, the prior rehearsal again unless it has been recorded.

Similarly, suppose a filmmaker discusses screenplay changes with the writer but does not document the modifications by recording, taping, typing or writing them. The changes are only ideas until they are written by hand, typed, saved on a computer or otherwise. At that point, the changes are fixed and can be perceived directly or through a device.

Other examples of tangible forms of expression include a motion picture, an on-set still photograph, a watercolor of a character in the film, a computer graphics storyboard, a recorded music score, a printed copy of a screenplay, a director's handwritten notes on a sticky pad, a social media post, a film poster, lyrics written on a cocktail napkin, and a design on a paper bag for a unique horror mask.

However, a table reading, a musical rehearsal, a dance session, an exercise workout, a stage play, the act of blocking actors and other such live activities are not fixed in a tangible form of expression unless they are filmed, photographed, recorded, sketched, or otherwise captured in a medium capable of perception directly or through a device.

By examining these criteria, you can determine what will and will not qualify for copyright, and if not, why not. Additionally, if you copy or use part of another person's copyrighted work, the new work you create is not "original." More importantly, your work infringes on the owner's copyright, subjects you to a lawsuit for damages and possible criminal proceedings. The exception is if you have the owner's written permission to use his work. Then your new work is a derivative adapted from the owner's work of authorship, which under certain conditions can be copyrighted. Chapter 5 discusses derivative works.

WHEN COPYRIGHT IS SECURED IN A WORK

At the moment that an original work of authorship is created and fixed in a tangible medium of expression, copyright exists and is secured in the work. Copyright exists in works of authorship even without registration with the U.S. Copyright Office. Copyright law makes registration optional for works created in the U.S. after March 1, 1989, although registration is still valuable and highly recommended.

The process of registration of a copyright is a formal legal filing with the U.S. Copyright Office that makes public the application and information about a copyrighted work, such as owner, title, type of work and more. The copyright registration process is simple and inexpensive and yields benefits that are not provided to unregistered works. Chapter 13 provides a valuable step-by-step guide and detailed information on online and paper form copyright registration.

PROTECTED WORKS

You know copyright protection exists in original creative works of authorship fixed in a tangible medium of expression. It is important to know what types of works of authorship are protected, as discussed below.

A variety of categories of original works of authorship may be copyrighted. This *Copyright Handbook for Films* focuses on films and related audiovisual works, including the sounds and music accompanying the works, as well as film-related design elements. Many other types of works can also be copyrighted, including:
- Literary works,
- Musical works, including the words that accompany the works,
- Dramatic works, including music accompanying the works,
- Choreographic works and pantomimes,
- Pictorial, graphic and sculptural works,
- Architectural works, and
- Sound recordings (independent of films and videos.

The USCO offers paper copyright forms, but encourages electronic filing, which is user-friendly and costs less than paper registration. Electronic filing is detailed in Chapter 13.

In the back of the book, you will find a Forms Bank that provides completed paper forms required to register a motion picture and a storyboard for copyright with the USCO. The filled-in paper Forms PA and VA have been completed using hypothetical scenarios of typical situations.

The form used to register a film with the USCO is Form PA for works of the Performing Arts, including audiovisual works and motion pictures, like films, music videos, workout videos, "making of" and "behind the scenes" films, corporate videos, and the like. Form VA for works of the Visual Arts is the form used to register a copyright in a film-related design, such as a storyboard, unique horror mask, tattoo, or art created for your film for which the designer signed a work-for-hire agreement.

If you hired an artist to create a unique design for your film and have this written agreement, the artist has assigned all of his rights in the design, including copyright. Therefore, you can register the design for copyright as the owner. Chapter 10 discusses many of the elements of a film that can be copyrighted separately from the film to generate additional wealth for the filmmaker.

Other primary copyright forms available for original works of authorship but not covered in this *Copyright Handbook for Films* are:
- Form TX, for dramatic works and texts such as for novels, non-fiction books, dictionaries, this *Copyright Handbook for Films* and computer software,
- Form SR, for works of Sound Recording, including music and lyrics or music only (but not film scores, which are copyrighted with the film using Form PA), and
- Form SE, for a single issue of a published or unpublished Serial, a work which is numbered or dated consecutively and is intended to continue indefinitely, such as issues of newspapers, magazines, professional journals and trade publications.

Additional forms are provided for other uses by the USCO on its website at www.copyright.gov. One form commonly used is Form CON for Continuation of a form for additional information such as the names and addresses of multiple authors. For more information on how to file for copyrights using either electronic or paper registration, see the step-by-step guide in Chapter 13.

UNPROTECTED WORKS

Copyright law does not protect all works. Some of the items, elements and materials are not protected by copyright include:
- Ideas,
- Titles,
- Names,
- Slogans or short phrases,
- Indecent or immoral works (determined by the USCO or a court),
- Familiar symbols or designs,
- Procedures or methods,
- Concepts, principles, discoveries or devices,
- Items of common information without any original authorship,
- Mere slight variations in lettering, coloring, or typographic ornamentation of items of common information,
- Lists of contents or ingredients, and

- Works that have not been fixed in a tangible form of expression.

While the above materials are not eligible for copyright protection, they may be able to be protected through other forms of intellectual property, such as trademarks, patents or trade secrets. The U.S. Patent & Trademark Office provides information on registering work for trademarks and patents at its official website, www.uspto.gov.

PUBLISHED vs. UNPUBLISHED WORKS

Original works of authorship may be published or unpublished. Knowing the difference is important because rights, including duration, of the copyright may vary according to the ownership of the work. The 1976 Copyright Act defines "publication" as:

"The distribution of copies or phonorecords of a work to the public by sale or other transfer of ownership, or by rental, lease, or lending. The offering to distribute copies or phonorecords to a group of persons for purposes of further distribution, public performance, or public display constitutes publication. A public performance or display of a work does not of itself constitute publication."

1. Published Work

A published work of authorship is one made available to the public without restriction on disclosure of the contents of the work. Publication generally occurs on the date in which copies are first made available to the public without such restriction. This is considered the "date of first publication."

The date of first publication of a film, for example, is the date it is distributed, or screened publicly for the first time to an audience with people other than just customary family and friends of the filmmaker. This publication could be a screening to the press, at a film festival, to distributors, on television, in theatres, streaming on the filmmaker's website, and other situations. Other examples of publication of films include uploading a film to a video website allowing public access without a password, sending a link to the film to an email list of potential distributors, mailing DVD screeners to potential buyers and a screening for a local charity. If a filmmaker offers the film to distributors, the film is published even if no sale is made.

For joint works, those by two or more authors, the date of first publication is the date the work was completed in tangible form after the final contribution by a joint author. In compilations or derivative works incorporating prior published material, the date of first publication is the date of creation of the compilation or derivative work.

Published works by nationals or domiciliaries in the U.S. that are protected by copyright may also be protected in a number of foreign countries that are signatories to international agreements with the United States. These agreements also provide copyright protection in the United States for foreign works to the same extent as protection granted to a U.S. citizen. Many countries in the world, however, have little or no protection for copyright. International intellectual property treaties and agreements are discussed in further detail in Chapter 12 in this book.

2. Unpublished Work

A work that is unpublished is one that is not made available or distributed to the public on an unrestricted basis. However, a work does not become published just by sending a copy of it to third parties. The key to an unpublished work is the copyright owner's restriction against copying, distributing or disseminating to any other party without the copyright owner's permission. United States copyright law protects unpublished works upon creation in the U.S., regardless of the home or nationality of the author of the work.

For example, if a filmmaker sends a link to his film to friends asking for comments and requesting they not send the link or show the film to anyone else without his written permission, the film is still unpublished. Though the film was sent to a large group of people, viewing was restricted with certain conditions and the film was not made available to the public.

DEPOSITS

Deposits for published and unpublished works, special deposits for motion pictures, and mandatory deposits are explained below:

1. Published Work Deposit

A "deposit" is a copy of the work of authorship. One or more deposits of a work are required with copyright registration. The owner of a published work of authorship, whether in or outside the United States, must file a deposit as follows when the work is registered for copyright with the USCO:

- In the U.S. before January 1, 1978, two complete copies or phonorecords of the work as first published,
- In the U.S. on or after January 1, 1978, two complete copies or phonorecords of the best edition, or
- Outside the U.S., one complete copy or phonorecord of the first foreign edition.

2. Unpublished Work Deposit

A deposit of one complete copy of the work or phonorecord is required for registering an unpublished work created in the United States after January 1, 1978.

3. Special Deposits for Motion Pictures; Literary, Dramatic or Musical Works; Three-Dimensional Works

A special deposit requirement is made for certain works, including motion pictures. For a published or unpublished motion picture or other audiovisual work, the copyright owner must deposit:

- If published, one complete copy of the best edition of the motion picture; if unpublished, one complete copy of the motion picture or identifying material, and
- A written description of the contents of the work.

The "identifying material" may be an audio recording of the entire motion picture soundtrack or one frame enlargement or similar visual print from each 10-minute segment.

For a literary, dramatic or musical work published only in a phonorecord, the copyright owner must deposit:

- One complete phonorecord of the work.

For three-dimensional works, the owner deposits:

- A photograph or drawing of the work.

4. Mandatory Deposits

By law, every author of a published work of authorship must make a "mandatory deposit" of the work within three months after publication, subject to narrow exceptions. This type of deposit is a copy of the work in physical form. Mandatory deposits may not be uploaded electronically, as explained in Chapter 13 in greater detail. The mandatory deposit must be sent to the Library of Congress, whether the work is registered for copyright or not.

The mandatory deposit for works published in the United States on or after January 1, 1978 consists of two complete copies of the best edition. An unpublished work created in the United States after January 1, 1978 requires no mandatory deposit.

If the published work is a phonorecord, the mandatory deposit consists of two complete phonorecords of the best edition and any printed or other visually perceptible material published with such phonorecords.

The deposit of a work submitted for copyright registration may serve as the mandatory deposit if the deposit of the work is made at the same time as the application and fee payment. In addition, if the work is copyrighted within three months of publication in the United States, any copyright deposit sent in physical form with the fee and application, together with any notice of mandatory deposit if applicable, serves as the mandatory deposit.

However, if the registration and deposit of a published work are submitted online, the actual physical deposit must also be submitted to satisfy the mandatory deposit requirements.

All deposits become the property of the Library of Congress and are not returned. Some exemptions from mandatory deposit are explained on the USCO website at www.copyright.gov. If an author fails to comply with the law, he is subject to penalties and fines.

POOR MAN'S COPYRIGHT

A popular copyright myth is that the "poor man's copyright" provides legal copyright benefits to an author. This refers to an author mailing a copy of his work to himself, not opening it upon receipt and relying on the postmark as "proof" of copyright.

However, the "poor man's copyright" serves no legal purpose at all. Copyright attaches to the work once it is fixed in a tangible medium without ever having to mail it. Therefore, the effort and expense of mailing is unnecessary.

WGA REGISTRATION

Registration with the Writers Guild of America West or Writers Guild of America East (collectively, "WGA") of written works, including screenplays and teleplays, is commonplace in the entertainment industry. For a fee, the WGA will accept a written work, assign a number to it and send a certificate to the writer. However, such registration does not provide any legal copyright protection to the author or owner.

Only USCO copyright registration offers the protection of legal copyright in the work and makes the work eligible for statutory damages and attorney's fees in an infringement suit against an authorized user, as discussed in Chapter 6 in greater detail. Below is a discussion of how to give notice to the public that a work is copyrighted.

NOTICE TO THE PUBLIC

An important aspect of copyrighting work is the use of a copyright notice. This is a symbol or text informing the public that a particular work is copyrighted and identifying the copyright owner. Notice of copyright also provides advantages in an infringement action, explained in Chapter 6.

A copyright notice is used on copies of works that are "visually perceptible" and can be seen. films and other audiovisual works of the performing arts. Audio recordings are not visually perceptible although many dramatic, literary or other works are fixed in audio recordings called "phonorecords."

The copyright notice on a phonorecord is different from other works of authorship." Copyright notice on a phonorecord is a capital "P" in a circle, followed by the year and name of the owner. It can be placed on the surface, label or container of such phonorecord.

For works other than phonorecords, such as films, copyright notice is placed on the work as a "legend," and includes the following three elements, in this order:

- An encircled capital "C" symbol, or the word "Copyright," or the abbreviation "Copr.",
- The year of first publication, and
- The author's name or other designation such as a pseudonym.

Under current copyright law, notice to the public on works created on or after March 1, 1989 is optional though recommended. The author should consider affixing the notice of copyright to his work before registration with the USCO. No permission or registration with the USCO is required for the notice, with one notable exception. Works created in the U.S. prior to March 1, 1989 are still required to have such a notice. Notice differs depending on whether the work is published or unpublished, as discussed below.

1. Notice for Published Works

Affixing a notice of copyright on a published copyrighted work warns potential infringers of the copyright and could result in statutory damages, often the highest damages for infringement.

A proper notice of copyright can take multiple forms. Examples of copyright notices for three different types of published works are: (i) by a company owning a work-for-hire work of authorship, (ii) by a

pseudonymous author, and (iii) by an individual using his legal name. These notices are shown below:
- Notice by a company:
©2021 Topnotch Films, Inc.
- Notice by a pseudonymous author using an alias:
Copyright 2021 Captain E-X-P
- Notice by an author using a legal name:
Copr. 2021 Jill Jacks.

Table 2-A gives examples of notices for published works on a work-for-hire basis, by a pseudonymous author and by an individual author copyrighting his work under his legal name.

Table 2-A NOTICE OF COPYRIGHT - Published Work	
Work-for-Hire	©2021 Topnotch Films, Inc. Copyright 2021 Topnotch Films, Inc. Copr. 2021 Topnotch Films, Inc.
Pseudonymous	©2021 Captain E-X-P Copyright 2021 Captain E-X-P Copr. 2021 Captain E-X-P
Individual Author Using Legal Name	©2021 Jill Jacks Copyright 2021 Jill Jacks Copr. 2021 Jill Jacks

As shown in Table 2-A above, the copyright notice date for a published work by an author or the owner of a work-for-hire is the date in which the work was first made public without restriction. The notice includes only the year of first publication, not the month or day of fixation.

Copyright notice to the public serves an important purpose. It notifies anyone who sees, hears, or has access to the work that it is copyrighted, the date of the copyright and the author of the work.

In practical terms, affixing the notice to a film, serves as a warning to others to refrain from using the work in an unauthorized manner without obtaining the copyright owner's permission.

Another valuable reason to affix a proper notice of copyright on the work is that an infringer is not "innocent" if he acquires the work or access to it in an unauthorized manner.

The innocent infringer defense reduces damages that would otherwise be due from a person who infringed on a work of authorship without knowing the work was copyrighted. With a notice to the public on the work, the proof of copyright is clearly in plain sight on the work itself.

Notices to the public for unpublished works are discussed below and displayed in Table 2-B below.

2. Notice for Unpublished Works

Unpublished works need no notice to the public unless they are distributed to the public. However, the notice serves a valuable purpose on registered works of authorship sent to third parties, notifying them the work is copyrighted.

Table 2-B provides examples of copyright notices for three different types of unpublished works: (i) by a company owning a work-for-hire work of authorship, (ii) by a pseudonymous author, and (iii) by an individual using his legal name.

Examples of notices to the public for unpublished works are listed below and in Table 2-B:
- Notice by a company:
  Unpublished work ©2021 Topnotch Films, Inc.
- Notice by a pseudonymous author using an alias:
  Unpublished work Copyright 2021 Captain E-X-P
- Notice by an author using a legal name:
  Unpublished work Copr. 2021 Jill Jacks.

The only difference between a copyright notice for a published work and an unpublished work is the addition of the words "Unpublished work" prior to the copyright symbol or word, date and owner's name.

Table 2-B
NOTICE OF COPYRIGHT - Unpublished Work

Work-for-Hire	• Unpublished Work ©2021 Topnotch Films, Inc. • Unpublished Work Copyright 2021 Topnotch Films, Inc. • Unpublished Work Copr. 2021 Topnotch Films, Inc.
Pseudonymous	• Unpublished Work ©2021 Captain E-X-P • Unpublished Work Copyright 2021 Captain E-X-P • Unpublished Work Copr. 2021 Captain E-X-P
Individual Author Using Legal Name	• Unpublished Work ©2021 Jill Jacks • Unpublished Work Copyright 2021 Jill Jacks • Unpublished Work Copr. 2021 Jill Jacks

COPYRIGHTED & COPYRIGHTABLE WORKS

Copyright is automatically created in a work and exists at the moment of creation and fixation. Even if a filmmaker does not register his film for copyright with the U.S. Copyright Office, the work is copyrighted when created if it meets all criteria for a copyrightable work.

Once copyright is secured and exists in a film, the filmmaker should place a copyright notice on it, even before publication and registration. Although optional for works created after March 1, 1989, this is still a recommended practice, requiring no approval from the USCO.

Ideas for future films that are not generic or scènes à faire and are original, creative and fixed in a tangible form are instantly protected by copyright as unpublished works. Persons and entities that can copyright and own a work, including a "work-for-hire" or sometimes, a "work-made-for-hire," are discussed in Chapter 3.

3. WHO

Who Can Copyright & Own a Film

This Chapter discusses the question of who owns the copyright in a work of authorship and, thus, who can register the work for copyright. The answer might seem as simple as the "author" or the "owner." But it is actually more complex. This Chapter discusses why authors and owners could be different persons and the reason for the difference.

The author of an original work of authorship is the creator of the original creative expression in the work. The author is also the owner of the exclusive rights in the copyrighted work, with one exception. If the author entered into an assignment agreement, the assignee or buyer owns the particular right or rights sold pursuant to the assignment.

If the author of a work is commissioned pursuant to a work-for-hire agreement or is hired as an employee per an employment agreement to create a work, the owner of the work is the person or entity that commissioned the work or the employer. Under copyright law, this owner is the author, not the actual person who created it. Whether a person is an author, owner or both depends on the agreement.

Who owns the copyright to a motion picture when so many people contribute efforts and creativity to the film? The answer depends on a number of factors. If the authors are employees of the production company producing and owning the film, the company is the owner as well as the author under copyright law. If the authors of the work are independent contractors providing services on work-for-hire agreements for a filmmaker, that filmmaker is the owner and author of all copyrights in the film.

Before ownership of the copyright in the film can be determined, it is important to know if any work-for-hire or other written agreements, contracts or deal memos have been signed. These can be executed in printed documents, digitally, handwritten notations or in any other form. An actual signed agreement by both the author and the hiring party best evidences the relationship.

When shooting a film, if no such agreements exist by the first day of principal photography, a filmmaker will find that his film is owned not only by himself or his production company but also by everyone who contributed original, creative copyrightable work to the film.

Authors, claimants, owners and agents are discussed below.

AUTHORS, CLAIMANTS, OWNERS & AGENTS

Sometimes authors, owners and copyright claimants are the same person or entity. Other times they are not, such as when the author is hired by, a third party to provide creative work on a "work-for-hire" contract.

It is important to know who owns a work of authorship because only that person or entity, or his authorized agent, can actually file the copyright application. The filer for copyright for an original work of authorship must be one of the persons authorized by the U.S. Copyright Office. These persons, described in further detail in this Chapter, are:

- The author,
- The copyright claimant,
- The owner of the exclusive rights, and
- The duly authorized agent of such author, claimant or owner.

Anyone in a category above that files a copyright application may be a single individual or might be multiple persons or entities.

A description of each of the four types of persons allowed to file a claim for copyright in a work for authorship is next.

- **The Author.** The author of a work may be either of the following:
  - The person who created the work of authorship, or
  - The employing entity or person who hired or commissioned the creator of the work pursuant to a work-for-hire agreement.

- **The Copyright Claimant.** A person who qualifies as a copyright claimant may be either of the following:

- o   The author of the work who is the original claimant, or
- o   A person or entity that has acquired ownership of all of the exclusive rights of copyright in the work that were originally owned by the author.

- **The Owner of the Exclusive Rights.** The owner of the exclusive rights of copyright in a work of authorship is one of the following:
  - o   A party who commissioned an author to create a work pursuant to a "work-for-hire" agreement, or
  - o   A person who acquires by assignment (purchase and transfer) all of the exclusive rights, as discussed in Chapter 5), or
  - o   A person who inherited the exclusive rights, or
  - o   A person who otherwise acquired legal possession of the exclusive rights as a transferee.

- **The Agent.** The agent who is qualified to file a copyright application is:
  - o   A person duly authorized to represent the author, a copyright claimant or an owner of the exclusive rights in filing the application, and
  - o   May be anyone authorized by such person or persons, which authorization should be in writing signed and dated by the author, claimant or owner.

The filer chooses under which name to file the work of authorship. The filer must certify under penalty of perjury that the information on the copyright application is correct. Any false declaration is subject to prosecution under federal law. A name can be one of the following:
- The legal name of a natural person as the filer,
- The filer's pseudonym, an alias or any other name but his own,
- Anonymous, where no natural person is identified, and
- The employer or party commissioning the work, if pursuant to a work-for-hire agreement.

Copyright ownership differs from on-screen credit in a film. The USCO does not have any authority over such credits. The writer, director, producer, editor, composer and all others providing creative efforts on the film on work-for-hire contracts receive credits as specified in those contracts. Although those creative professionals are the authors of their creative contributions to the film, they are not the owners of any of the exclusive rights of copyright in the works they create. All rights are owned by the owner of the film who commissioned the creative professionals pursuant to work-for-hire agreements.

A discussion about different types of authors follows. The first category is authors of works of authorship pursuant to work-for-hire agreements, including employment agreements.

1. Work-for-Hire & Employee Authors

An author may be commissioned as an independent contractor by a third party individual or entity on a "work-for-hire" agreement to create an original work of authorship within the course and scope of his job. The author may also be an employee of the hiring party, subject to an employment agreement.

Although the author creates the work, the person or entity that commissions or employs the author is considered to be the author and owner of the copyright in the work. Copyright law defines a "work-for-hire," sometimes referred to as "work-made-for-hire," in the following two categories:

- A work prepared by an employee within the course and scope of his employment, or
- A work specially ordered or commissioned for use as:
  - A part of a motion picture or other audiovisual work,
  - A contribution to a collective work, such as a magazine,
  - A translation,
  - A supplementary work,
  - A compilation,
  - An instructional text,
  - A text,
  - Answer material for a test, or
  - An atlas, if the parties expressly agree in a signed agreement that such work is considered a work-for-hire.

If a production company employs a director under a work-for-hire agreement to direct the company's film, the company owns the copyright in the film once it is fixed in a tangible form. The work-for-hire agreement gives all rights in and to the author's work to the company. The actual author does not have and does not retain any copyright in the work he created under the work-for-hire contract.

Often production companies or other entertainment business entities hire creative professionals as employees, rather than as independent contractors. The company requires every employee to sign employment contracts assigning to the company the results and proceeds of the employee's efforts, including, but not limited to, copyright. These employment contracts are additional examples of work-for-hire agreements.

To be the sole owner of the copyright in a film, the filmmaker must obtain a signed work-for-hire agreement signed by every person who contributes creative effort to the film. This agreement can be a one-page deal memo or a multi-page contract, but the purpose is the same. Under a work-for-hire agreement, the person hired for the film assigns the filmmaker all rights, including copyright, in the work he creates. This assignment is a full transfer of all of the exclusive rights in the copyright to the work performed on the film.

Suppose a filmmaker hires a writer under a work-for-hire agreement to write the screenplay for his film. The writer is the original author but not the owner of the script. In the writing agreement, the screenwriter assigns the filmmaker all rights, including copyright, in his writing services. By this means, ownership of the copyright in the script vests in the filmmaker.

As another example, a studio hires a director on a work-for-hire agreement to direct a film. Copyright attaches to every shot of the movie once fixed in a tangible medium of expression, whether film or digital. Additionally, copyright is secured in every edit of a film that is fixed in a tangible medium. Each revised cut that is saved or otherwise fixed in a perceivable form is copyrighted as a derivative work of the original footage of the film, which is a derivative adaptation of the script

Copyright also attaches to other work by the director in this example, such as storyboards, script revisions and editing decisions. Under the work-for-hire contract, the director is the original author of such work but the studio is the copyright owner.

A third situation where the author is not the owner of the rights occurs when an independent filmmaker sells his film to a producer, such as at a festival or market. The filmmaker assigns to the buyer all film rights, including copyright and its exclusive rights. Such assignment is a final sale and transfer of these rights. When the sale is concluded, the filmmaker no longer owns the rights and the assignee buyer is the new copyright owner.

2. Pseudonymous Authors

It is possible for an author to register his film for copyright without listing his legal name. He may use an alias, or a fictional name called a "pseudonym," instead of his own name. He registers his claim for copyright in the film as a "pseudonymous work."

Pseudonyms are used by filmmakers for a variety of reasons. As an example, Jack Smith usually produces horror films. He decides to produce a comedy but does not want to publicize that it is his. Jack decides to copyright the film under a pseudonym rather than his real name to register his work. The pseudonym can be any words and any number of words, so long as they are not names of people or entities protected under intellectual property laws.

Jack researches the U.S. Patent and Trademark Office ("USPTO") website for trademarks and verified that the three pseudonyms he devised are not trademarked: "Captain Experimento," "Smithyjack" and "Jack E-X-P." Jack can trademark those pseudonyms if he meets the qualifications for trademarks.

Names cannot be copyrighted but they can under certain conditions be trademarked. Federal trademark information is found on the USPTO, www.uspto.gov. Each state also has a trademark registration process and database of registered trademarks. Therefore, it is important to research both federal and state marks before choosing a pseudonym.

3. Anonymous Authors

Sometimes the author of a work does not want to register a claim for copyright under either his legal name or a pseudonym. Instead, he prefers to register without listing any type of name at all. In instances such as this, the Copyright Office allows the author to register anonymously. An "anonymous work" will be listed publicly on the USCO website displaying the author's name as "anonymous."

For example, if Becky Jones wants to register her film but does not want her name, or a pseudonym, found in the U.S. Copyright Office public records, she can file anonymously. However, the U.S. Copyright Office publishes the information in the application and contact information is required. To meet this requirement, Becky will list a third party, such as an agent, manager, attorney, friend or family member, as the contact for queries about her work. Therefore, she remains anonymous and the USCO still has a contact for questions about the filing.

It is important to list a contact in the public record to handle queries about obtaining one or more of the exclusive rights to the work. This could result in additional revenues for the copyright owner. See Chapter 5 for a discussion of these exclusive rights.

Another type of authorship and ownership is joint authorship, when a work is created by two or more joint authors. Joint authors are discussed below.

4. Joint Authors

Sometimes an author works with one or more other authors, all of whom wish to merge their individual works into one original work of authorship. These authors are "joint authors" or sometimes "co-authors" and their works of authorship are called "joint works."

When two or more joint authors contribute original work to a work of authorship and intend the result to be one original work of authorship, they are considered co-authors and co-owners of the copyright in the work. Joint authors typically share ownership of the copyright and the joint work unless they have a separate written agreement that states otherwise.

When a registration is filed for copyright on a joint work, each of the joint authors is listed as an author on the same application. No author files for a separate copyright on the same work. Not only does this eliminate uncertainty and confusion about the ownership of the copyright, but also saves the cost of multiple filings.

A joint work is not the same as a compilation, where one author collects and compiles works by different authors into one new work. Compilations and collective works, a specific type of compilation, are addressed later in the Chapter.

5. Minors as Authors

Subject to state laws, federal copyright law allows minors, that is, children under the age of majority, to file a claim for copyright. The U.S. Copyright Office does not regulate the business dealings involving copyrights owned by minors in any state.

Further information can be obtained from the relevant agency in the state in which you are interested. A starting place is the Secretary of State ("SOS") of the state in which you are interested. A list of websites for each state SOS or business officer in the U.S. and District of Columbia is listed in the Resources section of this book.

6. Foreign Authors

It is interesting to note that many works of foreign origin are registered and protected under U.S. copyright law. As an example, unpublished works by foreign authors, as well as U.S. citizens, are protected by copyright in the United States.

Some copyrighted works, which expired under prior U.S. copyright law, were revived by an international agreement among the United States and many foreign nations, called the Uruguay Round Agreements Act of 1994. Chapter 12 provides more information about this international intellectual property agreement. Additionally, if a work is first published by a citizen of a foreign nation with which the United States has an international agreement, that work is protected here under U.S. copyright law just as if the foreign author were a U.S. citizen. This is the same protection given to U.S. citizens' works in signatory countries of these international treaties.

COMPILATIONS

A compilation is a work of authorship in which preexisting materials are collected, chosen and compiled into one new work in such a unique or distinct way that a new work of authorship is created.

The compiler is the author of the new work of authorship. He can register a claim for copyright of specific characteristics of the compilation such as the organization, style, presentation and other such qualities. The materials assembled into the compilation may be in the public domain, as further discussed in Chapter 9. Alternatively, these elements might be copyrighted work, which the compiler has obtained written permission to include in the work, such as in a collective work.

However, obtaining a copyright of all of the materials contained within the compilation depends on the copyright status of each of the materials used in the compilation. The copyright in a compilation covers only the material that is contributed by the author of the work, not to any of the preexisting material used in the work, unless all materials are in the public domain.

Obtaining a copyright in a compilation does not affect, extend or reduce the copyrights in the preexisting material. One type of compilation is a collective work, as further discussed next.

1. Collective Work

A collective work is compilation in which a number of separate independent works of authorship are grouped together to form a new work by a compiler, who is considered the author of the work. A collective work is organized into a single work with the same title.

Examples of compilations include an anthology, magazine issue or newspaper edition.

The copyright on each contributed work in a collective work is distinct and separate from the copyright on the entire collective work. The owner of the copyright in the collective work acquires a license from the owner of each contributed work to reproduce, revise and distribute the contributed work as part of the whole collective work.

Film-related collective works include a film consisting of a series of short films by different directors, a book of on-set photographs taken by several crew members and a CD of musical scores on a particular style or theme of movie from multiple composers. Copyright secures in the collective work as a compilation for the way the work was assembled or other characteristics, but not for the individual works contributed. In the above examples, the copyrights to each short film, photograph and film score remain with their respective copyright owners.

DERIVATIVE WORKS

A derivative work is a new work of authorship that is based on, adapted from, or which transforms, preexisting material. The changes to the preexisting work in the transformative work must be substantial and original. If the work is only modified through grammar, punctuation, spelling or typographical errors or other editorial changes, the work will not qualify as a new derivative work for copyright.

If the preexisting work is still protected by copyright, a creator of a derivative work cannot obtain a copyright on his derivative work unless several conditions are met.

First, the preexisting material must be obtained lawfully by the author of the derivative work. No copyright will be granted by the USCO to a derivative work based on an underlying work that is obtained unlawfully. Some of the legal means by which rights can be obtained to create derivative works from third party rights include licenses, assignments, inheritances, donations or other means. See Chapter 5 for a discussion on the exclusive right to adapt or create a derivative work.

Second, in order to copyright a derivative work, its author must have contributed material that qualifies for copyright. That means the material must be original with some creativity and it must be fixed in a tangible medium of expression. The copyright in a derivative work will extend only to original material that is created by the author, not to any of the preexisting material on which the derivative work is based. No implied right to copyright of the preexisting material is given with any copyright granted to a derivative work author. It is also important to know that a derivative work may only be copyrighted with the written permission from the owner of the copyright to the preexisting material.

Last, the copyright in the derivative work does not affect the copyright in the preexisting material. That means the duration of the previously copyrighted work is not extended, nor are any rights of ownership of the copyright in and to the original work changed.

TRANSFERS

An owner of a copyrighted work may transfer one or more of the exclusive rights in the copyright to one or more owners. These exclusive rights and various means of transferring ownership of these rights, including voluntary and involuntary transfers are detailed in Chapter 5.

The USCO offers recordation of transfers; however, such recordation is optional. For the official proof that a transfer has been recorded, the new owner files the recordation with the USCO. This document becomes part of the official USCO public record. Fraudulent transfer recordations can be challenged legally and subject the filers to federal criminal proceedings for filing false information with the USCO under penalty of perjury, as well as civil liability.

In Chapter 4, look to the history and the law of copyright to learn why copyright is such an important asset to build a filmmaker's wealth in the entertainment industry.

4. WHY

Why History & Law Make Copyright a Powerful Asset

How did copyright become such a powerful asset? What is the legal basis for the strong copyright law in the United States? To answer these questions and understand the value of copyright for your films, look to the United States Constitution and the history of copyright law in the United States.

HISTORY

What the framers of the Constitution discussed before they enacted Article I, Section 8 of the Constitution is unknown. This Article embodies the "Copyright Clause," or sometimes, the "Copyright and Patent Clause." What is clear, however, is the interest of the founding fathers in promoting the expression of written ideas and discoveries by promising protection to the authors and inventors of these works for a limited period of time. The Copyright Clause issued in 1787 is the cornerstone of copyright law for writings, and of patent law for discoveries:

> "The Congress shall have Power...To promote the Progress of Science and useful Arts, by securing for limited Times to Authors and Inventors the exclusive Right to their respective Writings and Discoveries."

The framers offered a term of exclusive protection for those expressions to their authors and inventors. The original short term of copyright duration has been extended numerous times through the years to provide longer periods of copyright protection. In Chapter 7, you will find a more detailed discussion of this "duration" of copyright.

The Supreme Court has interpreted the meaning of the Copyright Clause in years of cases, defining terms such as "author" to refer not only to someone who creates "Writings" but also to a person who originates, or creates, a work. This Clause also protects discoveries of inventors.

Major differences exist between these two types of intellectual property and other forms of IP, including trademarks, service marks and trade secrets. They are summarized later in the book, which concentrates on copyright and providing tools to filmmakers to build wealth in the industry through protecting and copyrighting their works.

COPYRIGHT LEGISLATION

Because many copyright issues are specific to certain works of authorship, copyright information for films will often be different from that of music, or screenplays. The focus of this book is obviously films, though general information on other IP is provided later in the book.

Knowledge of copyright law is valuable for filmmakers. One main reason is that the basis of all wealth in the entertainment industry is Intellectual Property -- from screenplays and teleplays to motion pictures, television series, music videos, web series and more.

To build and keep wealth in this industry, a filmmaker must protect his IP against unauthorized use by third parties without permission. Such unauthorized use is known as infringement, and claims for such unauthorized use are governed by federal civil and criminal law. Chapter 6 discusses infringement and numerous legal remedies for damages including nine alternative methods to resolving infringement claims without filing a lawsuit and engaging in litigation.

The U.S. Copyright Office is the government office that reviews, approves or denies, and approves registration and protection of works for copyright. The various works of authorship that can be registered for copyright include motion pictures and other audiovisual works, storyboards, dramatic works, serial publications, sound recordings, lyrics, music, art, original designs, pictorial or graphic or sculptural work, photographs, computer software, and more. "Audiovisual works" and a type thereof, "motion pictures," are defined as follows by the USCO:

> "'Audiovisual works' are works that consist of a series of related images which are intrinsically intended to be shown by the use of machines or devices such as projectors, viewers, or electronic equipment, together with accompanying sounds, if any...the term 'audiovisual works' refers broadly to any work that includes any series of related visual images, whether or not moving, and with or without sounds, as long as a machine or device is essential to the viewing of the related series of images."

> "'Motion pictures' are audiovisual works consisting of a series of related images which, when shown in succession, impart an impression of motion, together with accompanying sounds, if any...[but] does not include the following: Unauthorized fixations of live performances or telecasts. Live telecasts that are not fixed simultaneously with their transmission. Filmstrips and slide sets which, although consisting of a series of images intended to be shown in succession, are not capable of conveying an impression of motion."

As in the definitions above, the type of media used is immaterial, whether film, tape, digital object or otherwise. A motion picture is a specific audiovisual work that gives the impression of motion, so this also includes works like video games.

A motion picture or other audiovisual work does not need to have an audio component, but it must have a visual component. Therefore, a silent movie qualifies, but a motion picture soundtrack alone does not as it is embodied in the film.

Subsequent to the Constitution, later copyright legislation has been enacted and amended over the years. Current U.S. copyright law is found in the United States Code, title 17, Chapters 1 to 8 and Chapters 10 to 12. The U.S. Code is a collection of federal laws and amendments to this legislation. The USCO website provides summaries and links to the law for those interested in greater details on the law, at www.copyright.gov.

This Chapter summarizes the most important laws affecting copyright films and other audiovisual works, found below. International treaties are covered in Chapter 13 in greater detail.

1. 1909 Copyright Act

The 1909 Copyright Act of 1909 was the U.S. copyright law from July 1, 1909 through December 31, 1977. This Act was amended by the 1976 Copyright Act as of January 1, 1978. Before this date, unpublished works were protected under "common law copyright," sometimes called "state law copyright." Certain works copyrighted under the 1909 Act for which copyright renewals had been filed by a certain date were extended by the 1976 Copyright Act.

2. 1976 Copyright Act

The 1976 Copyright Act comprehensively revised the 1909 Copyright Act, extending duration for many copyrighted works still valid or in a valid renewal period. For works created before January 1, 1978 not in the public domain, the existing renewal term of copyright of 28 years was extended by 19 years for a total of 47 years. When added to the initial term of 28 years, the total is 75 years. Thereafter the CTEA extended duration again for many works.

3. The 1998 Copyright Term Extension Act ("CTEA")

The Copyright Term Extension Act ("CTEA") of 1998 is sometimes referred to as the "Sonny Bono Copyright Term Extension Act" in honor of the late U.S. Congressman and partner in the famous Sonny & Cher singing duo. Congressman Bono was a sponsor of the legislation but did not live to see its enactment.

The CTEA extended copyright duration for an individual equal to European Union duration to the copyright owner's life plus 70 years. The Act also extended the duration of works by anonymous or pseudonymous authors or works-for-hire to the earlier of 120 twenty years after creation or 95 years after date of first publication.

4. The 2005 Family Entertainment & Copyright Act

The Family Entertainment and Copyright Act is federal copyright legislation enacted and effective in 2005. The law incorporates two separate elements, the Family Home Movie Act of 2005 ("FHMA") and the Artist's Rights and Theft Prevention Act of 2005 ("ART Act"). Some of their major provisions affecting filmmakers include that it:

- Legalizes technology allowing a home consumer to screen out multiple categories of objectionable content in DVD or Video on Demand ("VOD") content to the viewer, such as scenes showing drugs, sex and coarse or unacceptable language,
- Sets severe penalties for copyright infringement of motion pictures in a movie theatre, including a prison sentence of: (i) up to three years for a first-time offender, and, (ii) up to six years for a repeat offender, plus applicable fines, and
- Makes it illegal to upload a copyrighted motion picture or other audiovisual work or sound recording, among other works, onto a computer network where the public may access the work without the owner's permission.

5. Digital Millennium Copyright Act of 1998 ("DMCA")

The Digital Millennium Copyright Act of 1998 ("DMCA") updated U.S. copyright law to protect digital works of authorship. Among the main provisions are copyright owner "notice-and-take-down" provisions for removing unauthorized copies and posts on the Internet, Internet Service Provider responsibilities, penalties, and more. The DMCA is covered in greater detail in Chapter 11.

6. International IP Agreements

In addition to statutory legislation, the United States has entered into a number of international agreements relating to intellectual property protection with other nations. These agreements are called conventions or treaties and provide certain

copyright protections to U.S. copyright owners for their work in the signatory countries. Chapter 13 covers several of these agreements, including:
- The Berne Convention of 1888 and the Berne Convention Implementation Act of 1988,
- The Uruguay Round Agreements Act of 1994 ("URAA"), and
- GATT/Trade-Related Aspects of Intellectual Property Rights ("TRIPs") Agreement.

Additional IP laws enacted by the United States not discussed in this book that may be of interest are found at www.copyright.gov:
- The Copyright Royalty and Distribution Reform Act of 2004,
- The Satellite Home Viewer Extension and Reauthorization Act of 2004,
- The IP Protection & Courts Amendments Act of 2004,
- The Prioritizing Resources and Organization for Intellectual Property Act of 2008, and
- The Satellite Television Extension and Localism Act of 2010.

Other forms of IP in addition to copyrights are summarized below.

7. Copyright Alternative in Small-Claims Enforcement Act ("CASE")

See Chapter 17 for a discussion of this new legislation signed in December 2020 by President Donald Trump, which, among other provisions, establishes a Copyright Claims Board.

OTHER INTELLECTUAL PROPERTY

Filmmakers can benefit from knowing the basics about IP other than copyright. Even if copyright does not cover certain elements or materials of a film or a production company, such as a company name or logo, other forms of IP may protect those works. Some major differences between and among copyrights and other IP, including trademarks, service marks, patents and trade secrets are summarized below

Copyright protects original works of authorship. Patents protect inventions and discoveries. A trademark protects a word, phrase, symbol or design that identifies the source of the goods and distinguishes them from the goods of other persons or entities. A service mark protects the same for a service.

Trade secrets are confidential and proprietary materials and information kept secret by the owners to prevent third parties from gaining a competitive or economic advantage. Unlike the other IP receiving protection by U.S. legislation upon registration, trade secrets are not registered with an agency. However, theft of trade secrets is protected by law.

A filmmaker might access multiple forms of IP for certain works. For example, besides copyrighting a film he could trademark his logo for DVD sales, register his logo as a service mark for production services, and copyright the graphic design. If he uses one of his film characters in his business or to represent the company, he could trademark the character. He could also copyright a design of the character as work of visual art. He could even copyright and patent entertainment software he wrote or commissioned pursuant to a work-for-hire agreement for his company.

Applications for protection of IP through U.S. agencies are placed in the public record and revealed to the public. The exception is IP known as trade secrets. These are confidential and proprietary materials, data, processes and more, which are economic and competitive advantages of a company, not registered publicly but kept secret by their owners. Like other IP, trade secrets are assets and may be sold like property.

Anyone may obtain copies of public records through the federal Freedom of Information Act ("FOIA"), or equivalent state legislation allowing access to public records. Written requests are generally required and a nominal fee is typically charged for the government office to copy the requested records. In some jurisdictions, you are allowed to bring your own machine to copy records at your own cost.

For more information, see the U.S. Patent and Trademark Office site, www.uspto.gov, or the References section in the back of the book.

PART TWO

CAN YOU HANDLE THE TRUTH ABOUT COPYRIGHT?
Everything You Always Wanted to Know About It but Didn't Want to Hire a Lawyer to Do

5. EXCLUSIVE RIGHTS
The "Bundle of Rights" Builds Wealth

One of the major benefits of copyrights in a film is the "bundle of rights" that a copyright owner automatically owns when copyright in the work comes into existence. This bundle encompasses a group of exclusive rights wholly owned by the copyright owner, who is free to keep or dispose of them in a number of ways in his sole discretion.

These exclusive rights in the bundle of rights of copyright allow the owner to copy or reproduce, distribute, perform or display or adapt his work. You will learn how filmmakers, producers, directors and others can generate revenues by exploiting these exclusive rights in their works.

The owner of the copyrighted work is able to exercise some or all of these exclusive rights. Each right may be exploited separately and even divided by media, geographic territory, time and more. Thus, the owner can retain, sell, license or otherwise transfer, or authorize use of, each right on an individual basis without affecting the ownership of the other exclusive rights. Each exercise of each right also generates more profit.

A filmmaker can exploit his rights to generate additional revenues beyond one form of distribution, such as theatrical, streaming or Video on Demand. For example, a filmmaker could license his exclusive right to adapt or create derivative works from the film for specific works simultaneously to a book publisher, Broadway producer, television studio and foreign producer in another country for a book, Broadway play, television series or film remake in French, respectively.

Because the filmmaker owns the right to adapt his film as well as all the other exclusive rights, he holds IP assets he can use to build his wealth in the entertainment industry.

This Chapter also explains the various means by which a filmmaker who owns these rights can grant to a third party the right to use or own an exclusive right, thus exploiting the owner's rights in and to the exclusive rights in his film.

The filmmaker may exploit these rights through any of a number of agreements, including:
- Licenses,
- Sales and assignments (of one or more exclusive rights), and
- Options.

A discussion follows of the exclusive rights and means to exploit them to build wealth in the entertainment industry.

EXCLUSIVE RIGHTS

A copyright in an original work of authorship is more than just one right. Copyright contains a bundle of five exclusive rights for most works of authorship, subject to some limitations.

Copyright owners have the sole right to sell, or assign, or to license the use of any or all of these exclusive rights, separately or together.

Additionally, the purchasers who acquire one or more of the exclusive rights in the work may also license or sell them.

These exclusive rights are:
- The right to copy and reproduce the work,
- The right to distribute the work,
- The right to display the work,
- The right to perform the work, and
- The right to adapt and create derivative works from the work.

Exclusive rights may be restricted in several ways other than the expiration of duration, such as the doctrine of "fair use" and exemptions for reproduction and use by libraries and archives as discussed in Chapter 8.

A description of each of these five exclusive rights of copyright is found below.

1. The Right To Copy and Reproduce

The owner of the copyright in a film owns the exclusive right to copy and reproduce the film. That means the owner can make as many copies of his film as he wants. He can have made DVDs or digital versions of his film, including the accompanying audio tracks for dialogue, sound effects and music if the owner owns the rights or a license to use them. Owners obtain the rights to such services for films through work-for-hire contracts, discussed in Chapter 3, or through licenses, discussed below.

Some limitations exist on a copyright owner's exclusive rights. For example, an exemption is granted by copyright law to libraries and archives, to allow them to copy, reproduce and distribute certain copyrighted works without infringing. These institutions include non-profit educational institutions acting in such capacities.

Such institutions and their employees acting within the scope of their work are exempt from infringement for reproducing no more than one copy or phonorecord of a copyrighted work so long as:

- The copy is not used for direct or indirect commercial advantage,
- The collections are open to the public or available to all researchers, and
- The copy of the work includes the copyright notice appearing on the original work or a legend stating the work might be protected by copyright even if no such notice is found on the original work.

Additional exemptions limiting the exclusive right to copy, reproduce and distribute are also available to these institutions. For instance, the exempt institutions may reproduce a limited number of a published work if replacing a damaged, lost or stolen work in the collections of the library or archives. Other terms and conditions apply, and this exemption is strictly limited by law for purposes of preservation, scholarship or research.

The copyright owner also has the exclusive ability to distribute a work, described below.

2. The Right To Distribute

The right to distribute a work is exclusively owned by the copyright owner who may distribute copies of the work to the public by sale or other ownership transfer, or by rental, lease, or lending.

Distribution of a film can take many forms, including screening the film, licensing it for television broadcast, selling DVDs of the film, leasing them to libraries, posting links online and streaming the film for public viewing on the filmmaker's site, channel and other sites. Distribution by sale can take place in brick and mortar stores, eCommerce sites or at local markets, among other ways.

In addition to these methods of distribution, the filmmaker can give away DVDs of his current film to attract donations for his new film on crowdfunding sites. The filmmaker retains all the equity in his film, unless he chooses to access the new Securities & Exchange Commission Rules for equity crowdfunding, finalized in 2016 found at the website www.sec.gov.

Owners of film copyright can work with distributors to monetize the exclusive right to distribute. It is important to determine whether the distribution contract merely licenses the right of distribution, or other exclusive rights, or whether the contract is the sale of the exclusive right to distribute. If the latter, the owner will no longer own the exclusive right to distribute the film in any way or by any means.

However, this right can be licensed for particular territories, or for a limited period of time, or for a certain number of broadcasts or any number of criteria. A thorough review by an experienced attorney of the contract is very important prior to execution. The filmmaker should understand what rights, if any, he is selling and which he is retaining, as well as any limitations on any of the exclusive rights.

A lucrative exercise of the right to distribute is selling a film outright in a bidding war among interested buyers, such as at a film festival or market. A filmmaker has many opportunities to exercise his exclusive right to distribute his film, which should be exercised.

In addition to the right to distribute, a filmmaker also has the exclusive right to display his film, which is explained below.

3. The Right To Display

For the owner of a copyright in a film, the exclusive right to display the work publicly gives the filmmaker another tool to publicize and generate wealth from his work. This public display right is not granted for sound recordings, but is granted for the following works:
- Literary, musical, dramatic and choreographic works,
- Pantomimes, and
- Pictorial, graphic or sculptural works, including individual images of a motion picture or other audiovisual work.

U.S. copyright law defines "to display a work" as "to show a copy of it, either directly or by means of a film, slide, television image, or any other device or process" and "to show individual images nonsequentially."

This definition requires knowing the meaning of "copy" which copyright law defines as a material object "in which a work is fixed...and from which the work can be perceived, reproduced, or otherwise communicated, either directly or with the aid of a machine or device."

A direct display is hanging an original painting on the wall of an art gallery, home or other place. However, films cannot be "directly" displayed. Perceiving, reproducing or communicating a film requires assistance of a machine such as a projector or computer.

Displaying a film means showing nonsequential individual images to the public. Other examples of displaying works include images in a museum installation, club or other venue allowing perceivable views of the film.

Communicating the film through a machine or device means members of the public can perceive the display in the same place, or in separate places, and at the same time or at different times.

Displaying a work publicly refers to doing so at a place where a substantial number of persons, other than the filmmaker's usual circle of family and friends, are located. The right can be exercised by transmission, online uploads or otherwise to a place with a gathering of a great number of persons, other than the filmmaker's standard family and friends.

The right to display is different from the right to perform, discussed below.

4. The Right To Perform

A filmmaker who owns a copyrighted film enjoys a fourth exclusive right, which is the right to perform the work publicly. Copyright law defines "to perform" a motion picture or audiovisual work as "to show its images in any sequence or to make the sounds accompanying it audible."

Performing a film in public refers to performing the work in a place where a substantial number of persons is gathered, other than the filmmaker's usual circle of family and friends.

That means the film can be shown in theatres, uploaded online, streamed digitally, broadcast on television, on demand, or through any other device or process, which constitutes a public performance.

5. The Right To Adapt & Create Derivative Works

A copyright's exclusive rights are extremely valuable to a filmmaker and can generate additional wealth for the filmmaker if they are exploited to the filmmaker's advantage.

Although all of the exclusive rights can generate revenues for a filmmaker, the right, which can be perhaps the most lucrative, is the right to adapt the work and create derivative works from the original work.

Derivative works are works of authorship originating, or deriving material or inspiration from, a preexisting work to which new original material is added. The resulting new work of authorship is termed a "derivative work."

A filmmaker has the opportunity to exploit the exclusive right in his copyright to adapt his work for many things. Commonplace examples of derivative works from films include a book of a film's shooting script with on-set still photos, a television adaptation of the film, a Broadway play based on the film, a video game spin-off, and a remake, sequel or prequel to the initial film.

A copyright owner can grant a third party the right to adapt his work through various means. This right can be granted to one person or entity exclusively or to many people on a non-exclusive basis through a license, sale, option, or other means of transfer.

Filmmakers also have a lucrative opportunity to license the right to create derivative works from a film with a unique story and amazing characters. Designs of original characters in films, books, games, and other creative works may be protected by copyright as works of visual art as well as by trademark law, subject to certain criteria.

Derivative works of these characters take many forms, including toys, games, clothing, jewelry, food, restaurants and theme parks. Licensing merchandising rights of a filmmaker's copyrighted assets to third parties can generate substantial revenues while the filmmaker retains full ownership of the rights.

Examples of how to transfer one or more of the exclusive rights of copyright in a film are given below.

TRANSFERS

A film copyright owner may sell, license, convey or otherwise transfer his ownership in any or all of the exclusive rights to one or more persons or entities. The rights may be transferred in their entirety or they may be transferred individually.

Recordation of these transfers is optional with the USCO. An owner of any exclusive right through a transfer is automatically granted the protection and remedies as a copyright owner without recording the change of rights ownership.

Transfers can be voluntary or involuntary. The main types of voluntary transfers for copyrights as described below are:

- Licenses,
- Sales and assignments,
- Option and acquisition agreements, and
- Inheritance or bequests by will or without a will (intestate succession).

Transfers of copyrights can also be involuntary which are limited by specific statutory regulations. Involuntary transfers include government seizure or appropriation pursuant to law. How to make a transfer of one or more exclusive rights by license is explained below, followed by a discussion of how to transfer rights by assignment.

LICENSE

A filmmaker who owns the exclusive rights of copyright in a work of authorship can generate revenue and build wealth by signing a license granting third parties the right to exercise one or more of the rights.

A copyright license is a grant of rights by the owner to a third party to exploit one or more of the exclusive rights while the owner retains all ownership of the rights. The copyright owner is the "licensor" and the third party obtaining the license is called the "licensee."

The license specifies which rights are being granted by the licensor to eliminate overlapping claims or confusion about the rights. A license may be limited for a term, geographic region, or particular use. A license may be oral, though it is preferable to be in writing.

Filmmakers typically use exclusive and non-exclusive licenses. Copyright law also provides for statutory licenses, such as those for broadcast, and compulsory licenses for music. These licenses are discussed below.

1. Exclusive License

An exclusive license is an agreement in which a copyright owner licensor grants to a third-party licensee the sole authorization to exploit one or more of the exclusive rights of the copyrighted work under certain terms and conditions.

In a license, the copyright owner retains full ownership of the rights granted. However, the licensee is the only party that can exploit these rights, usually fixed for a term.

A licensee with an exclusive license will typically pay a greater price for the benefit of being the only one with the authorization to use or exploit the right. For example, a licensing right to adapt "all publications" from the film typically costs more than the right to adapt the film for "a book in Japanese" or "a remake in French."

If a distributor signs a license for the exclusive right to distribute the film "throughout the universe," the license is exclusive to the licensee. The copyright owner is precluded from any use and cannot grant other distribution licenses for the film.

Alternatively, if the license limits distribution to "Canada only," the license is exclusive in that nation only. This allows the copyright owner to license the film in all the other territories in the world.

The copyright owner granting an exclusive license, whether for a territory or the entire universe, or whether for one product category or more. In addition, the license terms should specifically state which rights are granted, their purpose, price and duration, and limitations on locations in which the rights may be exploited.

Copyright owners can maximize their rights from non-exclusive licenses as well. Non-exclusive licenses are discussed below.

2. Non-Exclusive License

A non-exclusive license is an agreement in which the copyright owner licensor grants one or more exclusive rights to one or more third-party licensees for certain uses as stipulated in the license.

Pursuant to a non-exclusive license, the licensee has certain rights to use the copyrighted work but without any exclusivity. In this arrangement, the non-exclusive licensee may not be the only one utilizing the right in a particular territory, or for a specific term or in certain media.

This type of license allows the copyright owner to maximize profit from the exclusive rights in the copyrighted work by licensing to a number of third parties. This license contrasts sharply to an exclusive license that limits the exploitation of a specific exclusive right or rights to only one licensee for certain purposes, territories, or time periods or any other criteria.

For example, a filmmaker that owns the film copyright may grant to each of several online video sites a non-exclusive right of distribution to exploit the film digitally on their respective online sites. The copyright owner could also grant non-exclusive licenses to multiple vendors to reproduce and sell DVDs of the film.

In either of the above examples, the copyright owner of the film is free to enter into other non-exclusive licenses for digital or DVD or other types of distribution. The licenses should specify the rights and limitations of the rights granted in such licenses. In this way, the owner is able to maximize revenues by licensing to multiple licensees.

A non-exclusive license allows the licensor to negotiate for the same rights with as many other licensees as the licensor wishes. This opportunity offers additional revenue sources for the exclusive copyright rights in a film and builds wealth for a filmmaker.

3. Statutory License

Copyright law provides non-exclusive licenses called statutory licenses for radio and television broadcasts and satellite transmissions of copyrighted works, among other purposes.

The USCO Licensing Division collects and pays copyright owners in some cases. On the USCO Home page, click the image, "Learn About Statutory Licensing."

4. Compulsory License

Compulsory licenses, often called "mechanical licenses" are automatic non-exclusive fee-based authorizations to make and distribute phonorecords pursuant to certain conditions, and to use certain copyrighted works in non-commercial broadcasts.

Some of the conditions required are:

- The owner must be the first to make a recording of the work,

- The person seeking the license must give a "Notice of Intention" to the copyright owner before any phonorecords or made or distributed, but no later than thirty days thereafter, and
- The person seeking a compulsory license must pay royalties directly to the copyright owner as set by the Copyright Royalty Board ("CRB"), discussed later in this chapter.

Compulsory licenses do not grant the right to use music in a film. Such rights are subject to negotiations directly with the copyright owners or their agents.

If the filmmaker wants to transfer one of his exclusive rights, or all of them, to a third party, he accomplishes this through a sale and assignment. This form of transfer of copyright ownership in one or more exclusive rights is discussed below.

SALE & ASSIGNMENT

The owner of a copyrighted work is free to transfer and sell one or more of the exclusive rights in the work. These rights may be sold as a complete bundle or they may be sold individually. They may also be divided up among several buyers.

A typical agreement used to transfer all of the exclusive rights (except "droit moral," or "moral rights," discussed earlier) is a written sale agreement, called an assignment or a sale and assignment, signed by the copyright owner.

Similar to a license, an assignment may be a sale limited to a certain use or a specific geographic location. The difference is that once the assignment is made, the copyright owner no longer has the ownership or use of the particular right, or the part of the right, being sold. However, the copyright owner retains ownership of all of his other rights, unless they are also assigned.

If the filmmaker sells all the rights in the work, he cannot use, license or sell any of the rights again.

Suppose a filmmaker who owns all the exclusive rights in his film signs an assignment agreement transferring the right to adapt the film into a stage play to a Broadway producer. The filmmaker has sold that right completely to the producer. The filmmaker cannot adapt his film for the stage nor grant anyone else the right to do so. That right is owned by the Broadway producer.

However, the filmmaker he is free to assign or license specific divisions of the right to adapt. He can transfer the right to publish a book based on the film, or to produce a remake, or to adapt the film for a television series or movie, or any other right to create derivative works based on the film.

If the filmmaker were to grant an exclusive license instead of an assignment to produce and stage the play for a limited period of time, the rights would revert back to the filmmaker upon the license expiration to exploit them again.

Another method of transferring rights is through an option and acquisition.

OPTION & ACQUISITION

A copyright owner also has the ability to enter into an option and acquisition agreement with a potential buyer of one or more exclusive rights of a copyrighted film. This type of agreement combines both a license and an assignment.

The option is an exclusive license allowing one party the use of one or more exclusive rights of a copyrighted work for a limited time. The acquisition is a sale and assignment that occurs if the optionee exercises the option and pays the purchase price to buy the rights.

The option portion of the agreement allows the potential buyer, the optionee, to pay a nominal sum for a limited period of time to fulfill conditions he needs prior to buying the rights. These conditions might include raising film financing or attaching cast before paying for the rights. Generally, the purchase price is fixed in the contract so that both the copyright owner and the optionee understand the costs and terms involved.

The acquisition part of the agreement occurs when the optionee has fulfilled the conditions he needs and exercises the option, acquiring and paying for the rights. When the exercise occurs, the copyright owner transfers the ownership of the right or rights in question to the buyer.

Often, the optionee needs more time beyond the initial option term. Option agreements generally include a pre-negotiated extension of the original option for a fixed sum to give the optionee more time to fulfill the conditions and acquire the work.

Filmmakers and producers often enter into option and acquisition agreements with writers for screenplays, paying a nominal payment up front for a fixed period of time.

For instance, a filmmaker signs an option with a Spanish producer for the right to adapt the film into a Spanish version. The foreign producer utilizes the term of the option to rewrite the script, raise financing, attach a director, cast and others, scout locations, and any number of other development activities prior to actually exercising the option.

An extension to the fixed option period is generally automatic by the optionee's payment of another sum of money, which may or may not be applicable to the purchase price.

An option allows the optionee to fulfill his contingencies without paying for the screenplay up front. If he is unable to raise financing or attach talent, for example, the simply lets the option expire and moves on to another project.

If the option is not exercised, the right to acquire the script terminates and all the rights granted in the option return to the author. This is referred to as the "reversionary right" or "turnaround" as the rights turn around from optionee and revert to optionor. At this point, the author controls all of his exclusive rights and he is able to option or sell the screenplay to someone else.

If negotiated in the option by the licensee, a subsequent buyer of the screenplay sometimes must repay the first optionee for development costs paid during the initial option.

The option and acquisition agreement is a valuable tool for a filmmaker to license rights to works of authorship and fix the purchase terms in advance without a large initial cash payment until funding.

The next section discusses the "first sale doctrine" which relates to rights of the purchaser of a copy of a copyrighted work.

FIRST SALE DOCTRINE

An important principal that takes effect when a buyer purchases a copy of a copyrighted work is the "first sale doctrine." This concept allows the buyer to do what he wishes with the legally acquired copy without the owner's authorization except exploit the exclusive rights.

The doctrine provides a limited exception to right to distribute. The buyer may purchase a film DVD and can then sell it at a yard sale or online. The buyer can discard the DVD or burn it. But the buyer cannot make copies of the DVD and give them away or sell them. Nor can the buyer upload the DVD online. That is the exclusive right of distribution, which is not acquired by a buyer of a copy of the copyrighted work without written permission of the owner of the exclusive rights.

The first sale doctrine does not apply to a person who merely rents or leases the work. Also, the doctrine restricts the buyer's right to exercise any of the copyright owner's other exclusive rights such as copying, displaying, performing or adapting into a derivative work.

The transfer of ownership in the material copy of the work does not transfer any exclusive rights to the buyer other than the right to distribute it.

The first sale doctrine allows the buyer to dispose of, or distribute, the work as he wishes, including selling, renting, leasing or otherwise distributing the work. However, the buyer is prohibited from copying or reproducing another copy of the work then distributing it.

A filmmaker's exclusive rights in copyrighted digital works are not subject to the first sale doctrine. For example, a buyer of a legal DVD of the film cannot distribute it digitally because that requires first making a copy, which violates the filmmaker's exclusive right to copy or reproduce.

If the buyer purchased a digital copy of the film, again the buyer cannot distribute the copy because uploads or other online transfers require making a copy, which violates that exclusive right.

Copyright owners may exploit all their exclusive rights themselves or they may choose to engage the services of a collective rights management organization, discussed below.

COLLECTIVE RIGHTS MANAGEMENT

The owner of exclusive rights of copyright in works of authorship can manage and exploit these rights by himself, pursuant to third-party licenses and through entities that manage rights, such as collective management organizations ("CMO"). A CMO utilizes its bargaining strength to negotiate licensing agreements, collect royalties and distribute payments to the copyright owners of the works who are members of the CMO.

Membership of CMOs is generally open to all owners of copyright and related rights, including authors, writers, composers, publishers, photographers, musicians, or performers.

Filmmakers can also join CMOs that manage certain film rights. Typically, owners of copyrights in multi-film libraries utilize CMOs for non-theatrical distribution of the films, such as video on demand, online streaming, club venues and bars. CMOs can be a useful tool to help production companies maximize their wealth.

Three film CMOs in the U.S. are Criterion Collection USA, Inc., Motion Picture Licensing Corporation and Swank Motion Pictures, Inc. A CMO handbook prepared by the World Intellectual Property Organization ("WIPO") and Baker & McKenzie is available at the following website: www.collectingsocietieshb.com.

COPYRIGHT ROYALTY BOARD

No administrative remedy has existed in the U.S. Copyright Office for screenwriters seeking damages or redress for infringement on their films. The USCO proposed a "Small Claims Court" in 2013 but no decision had been made to create such a vehicle with the USCO for infringement resolution of cases with low amounts of potential damages until 2020.

In that year, President Donald Trump signed into law new legislation that creates a Copyright Claims Board. See Chapter 17 for more details about the Copyright Alternative in Small-Claims Enforcement Act ("CASE").

A Copyright Royalty Board ("CRB") has existed, operating under the supervision of the Librarian of Congress, a Presidential appointee. The CRB is an administrative body in which three Copyright Royalty Judges determine the statutory rates of copyright licenses, such as for music or broadcasters, and distribute royalties to owners where applicable.

In addition, the CRB determines the compulsory licensing rate for qualified music use, including physical phonorecords, permanent downloads, ringtones, limited downloads and interactive streaming music. The CRB also handles royalty claims by copyright owners for cable, satellite and digital audio recording devices and media.

6. INFRINGEMENT
What About Unauthorized Use

Infringement is the unauthorized act of copying or reproducing, distributing, performing, displaying publicly or adapting into a derivative work a copyrighted work without the written permission of the copyright owner.

Sometimes infringement is confused with plagiarism. A person plagiarizes when he copies, uses or modifies all or part of a third party's original copyrighted work into a "new work" and presents this new work as his own. Many educational institutions and businesses have instituted policies prohibiting plagiarism. Numerous copy centers decline to copy a copyrighted work for a customer without written authorization from the author. And although plagiarism is a form of infringement, certain defenses may be available, such as fair use, explained in Chapter 8.

Infringement of films and other works of authorship occur in many different forms. Infringers, or alleged infringers, also have legal defenses at their disposal, which allow use of a copyrighted work without such written authorization of the owner, including fair use.

Without any justifiable legal defenses, unauthorized use of another's copyrighted work is a violation of a copyright owner's legal rights, including one or more of the exclusive rights in the bundle of rights belonging to him. Furthermore, such violation is illegal.

To litigate against an infringer, a copyright owner must have registered his work for copyright prior to any such infringement. An example of infringement is a person's secret filming of a motion picture at a screening, then copying the film and selling the DVDs without the filmmaker's permission. Another example is a person obtaining a DVD of a film, then uploading it to a peer-to-peer file-sharing site. Still another type of infringement occurs when someone copies several scenes from a film and reproduces them for use in his own film.

Any or all of these activities could infringe on a film, costing the filmmaker lost sales and allowing the infringer to reap profits without paying for the use of the rights of the film. These infringements violate a filmmaker's exclusive rights of copyright in a film. However, a filmmaker does have remedies. The types of infringers and damages they are responsible to pay if held liable for infringement of a copyrighted film by a judge, jury or arbitrator are discussed below.

TYPES OF INFRINGERS

The law distinguishes between two types of infringers. The first is a "contributory infringer" and the second is an "innocent infringer."

1. Contributory Infringer

A contributory infringer is a person who:
- Uses, copies or otherwise infringes, or induces or causes someone else to use, copy or otherwise infringe on a copyrighted work, or contributes substantially to such infringement without written permission of the copyright owner, and
- Knows or should know that the work is copyrighted.

A contributory infringer can be held liable for actual or statutory damages, attorney's fees and costs.

2. Innocent Infringer

An innocent infringer is a person who:
- Is induced or convinced by a contributory infringer to use, copy or otherwise infringe on a copyrighted work, and
- Does not know, and has no reason to know, that the work is copyrighted.

An innocent infringer may believe the work is not copyrighted because he has been influenced by a contributory infringer's words or actions. Or an innocent infringer may not know, and cannot be held to know, that the work is copyrighted.

Generally, the fact that the innocent infringer does not know the work was copyrighted is not a complete defense to infringement. He still committed the infringing act against the copyright owner's work and most likely gained a financial or other commercial benefit.

However, an innocent infringer can mitigate, or reduce, his liability for damages to the owner. Innocent infringers are usually limited to payment of their profits to the copyright owner but not statutory damages or attorney's fees.

The copyrighted work used by an innocent infringer bears a copyright notice that he can see, or should have seen, the innocent infringer has no mitigation defense. He becomes a contributory infringer who knew or should have known the work was copyrighted.

An owner's placement of a notice of copyright on a work allows a judgment of actual or statutory damages, attorney's fees and costs without mitigation to an infringer.

INFRINGING ACTS

Infringement takes many forms, includes direct or indirect actions of infringers that cause third parties to commit infringing acts, as well as the acts of those third parties. Additionally, each unauthorized use or copy of a copyrighted work is a separate an act of infringement.

For instance, copying a film DVD and selling it without permission of the filmmaker is an infringing act. So is uploading a copy of the film on a peer-to-peer site. In addition, filming a remake, prequel, sequel, translated film or other movie based on the original motion picture without authorization of the copyright owner is also infringement.

Whether an infringer obtains a copy of a copyrighted work legally or not is immaterial. The unauthorized use or copy of the work is the infringing act if the infringer knew, or should have known, the work was copyrighted.

An infringer can also be held liable for the further infringement by third-party innocent infringers who used or copied the work. To determine the number of acts of infringement, U.S. copyright law considers each unauthorized online download, streaming view or purchase of an unauthorized copy, and other means of infringement to be an infringing act.

If the work is a compilation or a derivative work, all the elements of such work is counted as one for purpose of infringement. Different types of film infringement, such as peer-to-peer ("P2P") file sharing, copying and selling DVDs, and using elements from a non-owned copyrighted work are discussed below.

1. P2P File Sharing

A common type of infringement is sharing digital files without the authorization of the copyright holder of the work uploaded or shared.

Consider this example of infringement on the film you made and screened to the general public. Your film displays a copyright notice following the credits. Jane obtains the screening and secretly films it, then loads the copy onto a peer-to-peer file-sharing site ("P2P") without your written permission.

A P2P site is a file sharing network where individuals on separate devices can access and distribute electronic files, many of which infringe on copyrighted works. Files may be shared or they may be accessed online through a technology protocol called BitTorrent, using a client computer program.

Jane can be held liable as a contributory infringer because she knew, or should have known, the film was copyrighted but uploaded the unauthorized copy to the site anyway. She can also be held responsible for all downloads of the file. Moreover, everyone who downloads a copy of the film from the P2P site is also an infringer.

Suppose four hundred people downloaded the copy that Jane uploaded. Each download is a separate act of infringement on the copyright of your film. The four hundred downloads constitute four hundred separate instances of infringement for Jane, the contributory infringer. In addition, each of the four hundred unauthorized downloads is one act of infringement by the person who did so.

Whether the people who download the film from the site are innocent or contributory infringers depends on whether they knew or should have known your film was copyrighted. If Jane did not edit out the copyright notice at the end of the film, the people who downloaded the film could be held liable as contributory infringers who knew, or should have known, the work was copyrighted because the notice of copyright is part of the film. Notice of copyright, also called notice to the public, is explained in Chapter 2.

Contributory infringers often eliminate copyright notices on copyrighted works. They produce covers for DVDs without notice of copyright and edit the notice from the film copy. Still, notice to the public serves an important purpose and can increase a potential damages award to the copyright owner.

2. Copying and Selling DVDs

In this example of infringement, suppose you produce films and sell DVDs of them to the public. Your notice of copyright is printed on each DVD cover and included in the credits at the end of the film.

Jay buys a DVD of your film from your online store, and then watches it. At that point, he knows, or he should know, the film is copyrighted. Even if he does not watch the credits at the end, he opens the DVD cover where the notice of copyright is posted. However, Jay has not committed any acts of infringement. He bought a legal copy of your film and you profited from the sale.

Then Jay sells the DVD to Bill without the DVD cover. Pursuant to the first sale doctrine, the sale is legal since an owner of a copy of a copyrighted work may dispose of the work how he wishes. However, he may not copy the work or sell the copies he makes. Those actions are infringing acts on your exclusive rights to copy and to distribute your film.

When Bill bought the DVD from Jay, he did not acquire any exclusive rights in your film copyright, including the right of distribution. Nevertheless, Bill distributed your film without your authorization by uploading it to a peer-to-peer website, where it was downloaded fifty times.

Bill is a contributory infringer who not only violated your exclusive right directly but also made downloads available to others, resulting in fifty additional acts of infringement, one per download.

Suppose you learn about the unauthorized upload of your film and locate Bill's address. You then send him a cease and desist letter. This is a written demand to stop his unauthorized use of your film and to pay you a certain amount for his unauthorized use and your damages. If Bill refuses to comply with your demands, you can proceed with numerous alternative solutions to resolve the issue.

3. Copying Non-Owned DVDs and Selling the Copies

The first sale doctrine discussed in Chapter 5 allows the buyer of a legal DVD of a film to sell, rent or dispose of it as he wishes. Thus, the owner of a legal copy has the copyright owner's authorization to exercise the right of distribution for the work. However, the first sale doctrine does not grant the same right to a person who does not acquire ownership of a legal copy of the work.

For example, Alex borrows a DVD of your film that was legally purchased by a friend. Alex makes copies of the DVD by either circumventing the duplication-prevention technology or otherwise and then sells the DVDs. He has infringed on two of your exclusive rights as the copyright holder -- the right to copy or reproduce and the right to distribute. Each time Alex copies the DVD he commits one infringing act, and each sale of a DVD is another infringing act.

Before receiving financial compensation for infringement, the copyright owner must prove the elements of an infringement case. These elements are discussed below.

PROVING INFRINGEMENT

The copyright owner, or plaintiff, must prove his case in a lawsuit or arbitration claim to obtain an award of damages. First, he must prove:

- He is the owner, providing a Certificate of Registration from the U.S. Copyright Office or other authentic documentation, and
- One or more original elements of his work were copied without his permission.

The plaintiff may have direct evidence of the infringement, such as an admission by the defendant or testimony of a witness who saw the infringing act. If not, he can show indirect proof of infringement that:

- The defendant had access to the work, and
- The defendant's work, or one or more important elements therein, is substantially similar to the plaintiff's original work.

If the copyright owner can prove his case, he is eligible for an award of damages. If the work was copyrighted within three months of publication and prior to the infringement, the owner may receive statutory damages and attorney's fees.

If the work is not registered for copyright as above, the copyright owner may be awarded actual damages of his losses and the defendant's profits, presuming the owner wins the infringement case.

If the copyright owner has registered his work for copyright and qualifies for statutory damages, he is not required to prove actual damages since copyright law establishes minimum and maximum financial penalties for infringement, depending on a judge, jury or arbitrator.

These damages are described below, followed by remedies available to the copyright owner for infringement.

DAMAGES

No one wants to learn that his copyrighted work has been used by a third party without the copyright owner's written permission. Fortunately, U.S. copyright law allows judgments of monetary damages to the owner of a work that is registered for copyright if he wins at trial.

If you prove your case at trial the judge, or the jury as the case may be in a jury trial, can issue a verdict in your favor and award damages. The amount and type of damages will depend on the facts and evidence proving the case.

Works must be registered for copyright to be eligible for statutory damages, attorney's fees and costs of court. Unregistered works or those that are copyrighted after infringement are only eligible for actual damages in a suit for the unauthorized use of such work.

Infringement is one individual instance of unauthorized use of a copyrighted work. If the infringer unlawfully copies a filmmaker's copyrighted film and uploads it to a file sharing site where it is downloaded by thousands, the result is thousands of infringing acts.

Unfortunately, the owner of an unregistered work cannot recover lucrative statutory damages and attorney's fees allowed by law for infringement on copyrighted work. Since infringement litigation attorney's fees can be expensive, it pays to invest in cheap protection of copyright registration available to all copyright owners for their works.

The owner of the work infringed upon may choose between statutory or actual damages, but not both, any time in ligation prior to judgment. The topic of actual damages is explained below.

1. Actual Damages

Actual damages are the amounts the owner of an uncopyrighted work, or a work not copyrighted within the required time period, is eligible for if he wins his trial. These damages are the total of the copyright holder's losses plus the profits the infringer earned from his infringing acts.

The copyright owner must show proof of the infringer's gross revenues to determine profit. The infringer may prove deductible expenses for the infringing activity to reduce the actual damages.

In this example, suppose you own all rights to your film and sell DVDs on your website for $20 each. A third party, Jenny, obtains a copy and sells 100 infringing DVD copies for $10 each at a farmer's market, earning $1,000 in revenues.

Table 6-A shows the actual damages that could be awarded if you win at trial against Jenny, the defendant in this example.

Your losses are $2,000, which is the total of 100 lost DVD sales at $20 per DVD due to Jenny's infringing DVD sales.

In addition, at $10 per DVD, the defendant has earned $1,000, less her expenses for the sales of the 100 infringing DVDs.

As can be seen on Table 6-A, your actual damages would be $3,000, calculated by adding the total of your lost sales of $2,000 and the $1,000 in profits earned by Jenny.

Table 6-A ACTUAL DAMAGES - 100 ACTS LOST SALES & PROFITS		
Actual Damages Description	Actual Damages 100 Acts	How Calculated
Copyright Owner's Losses (Lost Sales)	$2,000.00	100 lost DVD sales at $20.00 each
Defendant's Profits	$1,000.00	Profits for 100 DVD sales at $10.00 each
TOTAL ACTUAL DAMAGES	$3,000.00	Owner's Lost Sales and Defendant's Profits

In many cases, actual damages are difficult to prove and the profits earned are usually unknown. The infringer may not have financial records or may claim to, or may have, lost them. It may be impossible to calculate total financial injury caused by infringing acts to the copyright owner and his licensees. But owners of registered works qualify for statutory damages, discussed below.

2. Statutory Damages

Statutory damages are financial damages fixed by law as compensation to a registered copyright owner for third-party infringement on his work if the infringement is proven in trial.

Current statutory damages range from $750 up to $30,000 *per infringement*. That amount can be increased to $150,000 *per infringement* if the court finds that the infringer acted willfully in infringing on the copyrighted work.

In addition to other evidence that may prove willful infringement, the law presumes the defendant acted willfully if the plaintiff proves the defendant provided or caused the provision of false contact information to register, maintain or renew a domain name used in connection with the infringement. The defendant can offer evidence to disprove this presumption, however.

Statutory damages for multiple acts can be substantial. Below, Table 6-B compares an award for statutory damages for one act of infringement with an award for 100 acts of infringement of the exclusive rights of copyrighted works.

Table 6-B
STATUTORY DAMAGES - 1 vs. 100 ACTS

Statutory Damages per Infringement	Damages for 1 infringing Act	Damages for 100 Infringing Acts
$750.00 minimum	$7,500.00	$750,000.00
$30,000.00 maximum	$30,000.00	$3,000,000.00
$150,000.00 if Willful Infringement	$150,000.00	$15,000,000.00

As seen in Table 6-B, one act yields statutory damages of $7,500, compared to $750,000 for 100 acts of infringement. The total increases to $150,000 for one act of willful infringement compared to $15 million for 100 acts.

In addition to statutory damages, a copyright owner whose registered work is infringed upon is eligible for attorney's fees if he prevails in the case, as seen below.

3. Attorney's Fees

The owner of a published work registered within three months after publication, or prior to infringement for an unpublished work, is eligible for attorney's fees if he prevails in an infringement lawsuit. Whether the trial attorney's fee agreement is a contingency fee based on recovery of damages, or hourly or other legal fees, the defendant ordered to pay is responsible for these fees. If the work was not registered for copyright, actual damages but no attorney's fees may be awarded to the plaintiff who wins an infringement suit.

4. Costs

In an infringement lawsuit, the court may issue a judgment to the party who wins the trial that the other party reimburse him for all his costs. These include, without limitation, court filing fees, depositions, expert witness fees, and more.

COMPARE STATUTORY vs. ACTUAL DAMAGES

To calculate how quickly statutory damages can increase with multiple acts of infringement, consider the following example. Harry copies your film from a DVD he borrows from a friend and he reproduces the DVD and sells 100 copies for $10 each. Unfortunately, the DVD has no Digital Rights Management ("DRM") software imbedded to prevent unauthorized copying. Learn more about DRM in Chapter 11.

Harry's hundred DVD sales constitute 100 acts of infringement by him as a contributory infringer, not just one infringing act of copying your film without permission. If you file an infringement suit for the infringing acts on your registered film and win, the court may order Harry to pay the lowest statutory damages allowed of $750 per infringement. Statutory damages are calculated by multiplying the per infringement amount of $750 times 100, the number of infringing acts. Total statutory damages would be $75,000, before attorney's fees or costs.

However, the judge could find willful infringement if he believes Harry infringed on the work knowing it was copyrighted. The damage award could be $150,000 *per infringement*, which would make the total statutory damages $15 million, which is the total of $150,000 times 100 acts, before adding in attorney's fees and costs.

Table 6-C below shows a comparison between statutory damages and actual damages based on the foregoing hypothetical case.

Damages per Infringement	Statutory Damages for 100 Acts	Actual Damages	Difference Statutory vs. Actual Damages
Copyright Owner's Lost Sales plus Defendant's Profits		$3,000.00	
Statutory minimum $750.00 per act	$75,000.00		$72,000.00
Statutory maximum $150,000.00 per act	$15,000,000.00		$14,997,000.00

Table 6-C
STATUTORY vs. ACTUAL DAMAGES - 100 ACTS

Compare the statutory damages awards with a judgment for actual damages, rather than statutory damages. In the prior example, Harry sold 100 infringing DVD's of your film and made $1,000, while you lost $2,000 in DVD sales due to Harry's infringement. The total of your losses added to Harry's profits results in actual damages of $3,000, before costs and attorney's fees. The difference is astounding between your actual damages of $3,000 and potential statutory damages ranging from $75,000 up to $15 million.

The owner of a work registered with the USCO can also receive attorney's fees in addition to either actual damages or statutory damages. Whether the lawyer charges a percentage of the amount of damages awarded or an hourly rate plus expenses, attorney's fees in an infringement lawsuit could be substantial.

With the cheap protection of online copyright registration as low as a $35 (slightly more for paper filings by mail), a copyright owner is eligible for awards after winning at trial of statutory damages and attorney's fees for infringement on his copyrighted work during his lifetime. The owner's heirs of his work are also protected for 70 years from the author's death without additional fees unless they choose to file an optional notice of transfer of ownership.

A copyright owner can choose either actual damages or statutory damages at any time during a trial prior to judgment. This allows the owner the opportunity to review evidence presented and determine which type of damages is more beneficial to him. However, if the owner loses at trial, he receives no damages and may be ordered to pay the defendant his costs for the trial.

Fortunately, a copyright owner whose rights have been infringed can implement a number of methods to resolve the infringement issue.

REMEDIES & RESOLUTIONS

To file a lawsuit for infringement on all works of authorship of U.S. origin and be eligible for statutory damages and attorney's fees, copyright registration of the work with the USCO is required.

Once a copyright owner discovers that a third party has infringed on his copyright, he should first verify that he is the registered owner of the copyright by researching the official records of the USCO. If he is the owner of the copyright in the USCO records, the copyright owner may file suit in a federal court. A guide to USCO record research is in Chapter 14.

If a copyright owner's work is infringed, the owner as plaintiff may file suit against the infringer, the defendant. Federal law governs copyright claims so litigation must be filed in Federal District Court. The case proceeds pursuant to the Federal Rules and Rules of Evidence, with a magistrate judge who handles certain preliminary matters or more if the parties agree, and a federal judge. The plaintiff may ask the court that the defendant be ordered to do the following:

- To stop the infringement (through court orders called injunctions), and
- To pay money damages (actual damages or statutory damages and attorney's fees and costs).

Prior to litigation, the owner should send a cease and desist letter.

1. Cease and Desist Letter

If a copyright owner has a physical or email address for an infringer, the owner can send a "cease and desist" letter to the infringer. This is a written communication to inform the third party of the copyright owner's rights and of his intention to enforce his legal rights. The letter might also contain a demand for payment for past infringement, offer a license agreement to cover past infringement and future use, or threaten litigation if the infringing acts do not stop.

A cease and desist letter may be effective in resolving infringement early without the time and expense of other alternatives, such as litigation or Alternative Dispute Resolution.

2. Civil Litigation

A copyright owner has several litigation remedies available against an infringing defendant. The owner, the plaintiff in the case, may demand damages and attorney's fees, costs, an injunction, impoundment or seizure, and destruction of the infringing articles.

- **Litigation for damages, attorney's fees and costs.** A copyright owner who registered his copyright with the USCO within three months of its publication can sue in federal district court and be eligible for an award of statutory damages, attorney's fees and costs. If the work is unpublished, the work must have been registered before the infringement occurs in order to qualify for statutory damages and attorney's fees. The copyright owner plaintiff must prove his work was original, creative and fixed in a tangible medium of expression. If he wishes to recover statutory damages, attorney's fees and costs, he must have a Certificate of Registration or other proof or registration with the USCO.

The plaintiff must also prove the defendant had access to the work, or the defendant may claim the infringing work is merely a similarity or coincidence as an independent creation, a defense to infringement. If the work is unpublished, the plaintiff must show how the defendant had access to or obtained a copy of the copyrighted work. If a copyright owner proves that the infringer acted willfully, statutory damages increases up to $150,000 per act, rather than a range of $750 to $30,000 per infringing act. The owner of a work that has not been registered for copyright can sue for actual damages, which are the total of his losses and the defendant's profits from the infringing use.

- **Injunction.** Plaintiffs who file copyright claim lawsuits may also file a motion asking the court to issue an injunction. This is a court order issued to the defendant to stop the infringing act or acts. The injunction may be preliminary, which is valid for a limited period of time. Alternatively, the order may be final, which is permanent and does not expire unless challenged in a court filing. Any court with jurisdiction over the federal civil lawsuit filed for infringement can issue a preliminary, or temporary short-term injunction, or a final, permanent injunction. Either type may be served anywhere in the United States on the person ordered to stop his acts, not just in the state where the court granted this order. If the infringer refuses to obey an injunction when served, it can be enforced by contempt of court or other means.

- **Impoundment and Destruction of Infringing Articles.** Impoundment means the seizure of the items that infringed on the copyright owner's exclusive rights. While a civil lawsuit for damages is pending, the court may order the impounding and destruction of the infringing items. For example, if infringing DVDs of your film were seized, they, as well as any negatives or "originals" of the film in any form or media, could be destroyed without compensation to the infringer.

Although a plaintiff can represent himself in federal court without a lawyer on a "pro se" basis, generally an inexperienced plaintiff unfamiliar with intellectual property law or the Federal Rules could find the experience daunting. Additionally, federal litigation is costly. The USCO has estimated costs of approximately $350,000 for a federal copyright claim litigation valued at under $1 million. The costs increase if an appeal of the trial verdict is filed.

A cost-efficient option to litigation is Alternative Dispute Resolution ("ADR") to resolve infringement, discussed below.

3. Alternative Dispute Resolution ("ADR")

Instead of litigation, a copyright owner can elect one or more Alternative Dispute Resolution ("ADR") methods to settle conflicts with an infringer. Five ADR methods are discussed below, followed by four additional means of handling copyright infringement, including criminal proceedings by a federal prosecutor.

- **Mediation.** In the ADR procedure of mediation, a neutral third party assists the disputing parties to resolve differences, usually without evidence or witnesses. The neutral is usually an ADR-trained lawyer, whose fee is split between the parties. The parties do not need lawyers although in larger disputes, attorneys and forensic accountants usually represent claimants and defendants to discuss financial analysis with the mediator.

    Typically, each party makes a statement of his case before separating into different rooms from each other. The mediator meets with each party individually, assesses the value of their claim, and assists the parties to a resolution rather than making a decision in the matter. To reach resolution, the copyright owner may reduce his damage claim or forego other demands, while the infringer may do or pay more than planned. If an agreement is reached, the parties sign a binding contract for their obligations to each other. Either party is free to sue the other if he fails to comply with the agreement.

Mediation is voluntary, unless a mediation clause is required in the parties' contract. The process is an efficient way to settle disputes and is a low-cost method for filmmakers to resolve conflicts without court or other remedies.

- **Arbitration.** Arbitration is an ADR proceeding similar to a trial, though more informal. The parties may choose a neutral organization to supervise the arbitration. A party may present his own case or be represented by an attorney. Rules regarding discovery, evidence, experts, witness testimony and other issues are set forth and implemented by the supervisory organization.

  The disputing parties mutually agree on one or more neutral parties to supervise the arbitration and to issue a final determination and an award. Many organizations require such arbitration to be binding so that this ADR proceeding fully and completely resolves all issues between the parties.

  For smaller claims, usually under $100,000 or even less, these ADR organizations typically offer expedited, streamlined arbitration, which is quicker and lower in cost than more complex arbitration involving greater damages claims.

- **Guild Arbitration.** Filmmakers and production companies in the entertainment industry that are signatories to entertainment Guild collective bargaining agreements are subject to the arbitration clauses in those agreements. Several Guilds with arbitration clauses in their agreements include the Directors Guild of America, SAG/AFTRA and the Writers Guild of America.

  Non-signatories to these collective bargaining agreements do not work with Guild rules, but engage other organizations for arbitration. The References section in the back of the book provides contact information for a number of Guilds and unions as well as third-party ADR organizations. Three major ADR providers are discussed below.

- **Private ADR Providers and Remedies.** Entertainment industry professionals and companies that are not bound to Guild or union arbitration clauses often choose a private organization as neutral administrators of entertainment disputes. Procedures these organizations administer may include mediation, binding arbitration, settlement conferences, neutral expert or other analysis, mini-trials and discovery settlements.

  To proceed with any mediation or arbitration, the parties in the dispute must select the mediator or arbitrator and agree to the proceeding, the rules of the ADR organization and the forum, or location where the proceeding is to take place. For arbitrations, the parties must also agree whether the decision reached by the arbitrator or arbitrator panel will be "final and binding." If so, suit may be filed to enforce the decision. If not, the parties are free to litigate or choose other methods to resolve the dispute. Three major private ADR providers are:

  - **IFTA Arbitration™**: The Independent Film & Television Alliance ("IFTA"), formerly the American Film Marketing Association ("AFMA"), a global non-profit trade association of distributors and producers of independent film and television productions, offers mediation and arbitration services with IFTA rules for IFTA members and non-members relating to disputes in production, finance and distribution. The website is www.ifta-online.org.

  - **JAMS**: JAMS is the largest ADR provider in the world offering ADR administration procedures for disputes in many fields, including entertainment and intellectual property cases and also holds numerous complimentary workshops. The JAMS website is www.jamsadr.com.

  - **American Arbitration Association™**: This ADR organization has numerous offices inside and outside of the United States and offers dispute resolution administration for intellectual property, entertainment and many other types of cases. The website is adr.org

- **Mediation/Arbitration.** The combination of both mediation and arbitration as ADR is often used by entertainment professionals and other companies to resolve disputes. Using this method, the parties attempt to mediate with a jointly chosen neutral who attempts to navigate them toward a solution. If this procedure is unsuccessful, the parties then commence arbitration. It is highly recommended to engage a different neutral than the mediator to serve as arbitrator who can approach and decide the case without having prior knowledge of the dispute or the parties.

4. Restitution

In restitution, the infringer pays the copyright owner an agreed-upon amount to compensate for the owner's losses, the infringer's profits, both or a different amount. The parties sign an agreement with conditions for future use. A party can sue on the restitution agreement if the other party fails to honor the agreement.

Even if restitution is made immediately upon agreement, the parties generally sign an agreement ending the dispute and all claims between the parties. The document should detail the copyrighted work and that for specified consideration made by one party and received by the other, the parties have terminated all claims and disputes between them relating to the specific work.

5. License

The copyright owner may grant an exclusive or non-exclusive license for past or current infringement, and for future use:

- **Exclusive License.** The copyright owner may grant an exclusive license for one or more of the exclusive rights to the copyrighted work. This license may be retroactive to the date of infringement and require payment for past-unauthorized use before future use is allowed, or not. After granting an exclusive license for an exclusive right to the infringer licensee, the owner may not use the right nor grant it to others until the license expires unless the exclusive right is divided, such as by use, territory, time period or otherwise.

- **Non-Exclusive License.** A copyright owner may grant a non-exclusive license to the infringer for prior infringing acts and for future use of one or more exclusive rights. A non-exclusive licensee is not the only person who has the right to exploit such rights. The owner may do so himself, and he may also grant the same right to others pursuant to a non-exclusive license.

6. Assignment

Copyright owners may also sign a sale and assignment of one or more exclusive rights to the infringer. In this way, the owner is compensated and the infringer obtains the rights he wants for his activities, usually of a commercial nature. Because the ownership of the exclusive right or rights is assigned and transferred to the infringer, the copyright owner no longer has authorization to exploit such rights or to grant their exploitation to anyone else.

7. WIPO International Dispute Resolution

The World Intellectual Property Organization ("WIPO") offers a neutral forum to resolve disputes outside court in these three ways:

- **Mediation.** WIPO mediation facilitates a mutually agreeable resolution between parties through the mediation process conducted by an impartial third party.

- **Arbitration.** In WIPO arbitration, an impartial third party reviews the dispute and issues a decision and award to settle the conflict. The parties decide in advance if the decision will be final and binding to resolve the case, or if they reserve rights to other resolutions, including litigation.

- **Expert Determination.** When the parties disagree on an issue in their dispute, they may agree to hire one or more experts to determine answers to specific issues, including copyright value or technical questions.

8. U.S. Customs Service

A valuable but lesser-known benefit of copyright registration with the USCO is the ability to record it with the U.S. Customs Service. This is a means of protecting the copyright owner against third-party imports of infringing copies of the copyrighted work, sometimes called "gray market goods" or "counterfeit goods." For more information, visit the website, www.cpb.gov.

CRIMINAL PROCEEDINGS

Infringement of a copyrighted work by an infringer who willfully infringes under certain conditions is a criminal offense punishable by law under title 18 of the United States Code. Punishment may include imprisonment for a term up to ten years, fines, destruction of infringing articles, restitution or other options in addition to any other benefits to the owner. Below are types of criminal issues and remedies arising out of certain infringing acts.

1. Willful Infringement & Evidence

Criminal charges may be filed against a person who willfully commits an unauthorized infringing act of a copyrighted work:
- For private financial gain or commercial advantage,
- By distributing or reproducing the work including by electronic means, one or more copies or phonorecords or one or more copyrighted works with a total retail value of more than $1,000 during any 180-day period,
- By distributing a work in the process of being prepared for commercial distribution through making it available on a

computer network accessible to the public, if the person distributing the work knew or should have known the work was intended, or being prepared, for commercial distribution. The work may be a motion picture or other audiovisual work if at the time of the unauthorized distribution the copyright owner has a reasonable expectation of distributing the film commercially but has not yet commercially distributed copies of the work, and
- If a motion picture is made available for viewing in a motion picture exhibition facility but has not yet been publicly available for sale when the unauthorized distribution occurs.

2. Fraudulent Removal of Copyright Notice

If a person has fraudulent intent and removes or changes any notice of copyright on a copyrighted work, the person shall be fined no more than $2,500 pursuant to law.

3. Fraudulent Notice of Copyright

If a person with fraudulent intent knowingly puts a false notice of copyright or wording to that effect on any item, or imports for public distribution or publicly distributes items with such notice or wording he knows is false he shall be fined no more than $2,500.

4. False Representation

A person who knowingly makes a false representation of a material fact in a registration application for copyright or in any written statement sent in relation to the application, by any means including electronic, shall be fined no more than $2,500.

5. Restitution

The defendant may also be ordered to pay restitution for the owner's actual damages, losses and/or the defendant's profits.

A defendant in an infringement suit may assert a number of defenses, discussed in the next section.

DEFENSES

In a civil or criminal proceeding, the defendant can employ several legal defenses that justify his unauthorized use and preclude liability for damages on an infringement claim including the following:

1. Statute of Limitations

The statute of limitations in copyright law set the time limit for filing a civil infringement action to three years after the infringement occurred, and to five years for a criminal action. Courts may consider civil claims for infringing acts that continue past the barred period into the three years immediately preceding a filing.

2. Fair Use

Copyright law allows a fair use defense to infringement, subject to U.S. Supreme Court guidelines for activities such as criticism, comment, news reporting, scholarship and research, in Chapter 8.

3. Exceptions

Exceptions to infringement for libraries and archives allow copying of copyrighted work to replace lost or deteriorated works, after a reasonable investigation that the work is not commercial exploited and a copy is not available at a reasonable price.

4. Public Domain

Works for which copyrights have expired or for which no IP are owned exist are in the "public domain" free for anyone to use. Use of a public domain work is a defense to infringement.

5. License

A defendant's exclusive or non-exclusive license for exclusive rights from the owner is a defense against infringement.

6. Ownership of Exclusive Rights

Any defendant who acquires an exclusive right of copyright can claim the defense of ownership by proving he owns such right or rights by a written sale, transfer, inheritance or other means executed by the former copyright owner and the defendant.

7. Independent Creation

A person accused of infringing may put forth the legal defense of "independent creation." This means that the alleged infringer claims that he created his own original work, or one or more elements within his work that is substantially similar to the work of the copyright owner claiming infringement. For example, a filmmaker in London may produce a movie similar to yours. He would defend any claim of infringement by proving his work is his original independent creation, typically with records such as a story synopsis, treatment, beat sheet, storyboards and witnesses. Record-keeping is crucial.

8. Digital Safe Harbors

The DMCA grants certain "safe harbor" infringement exemptions to qualified online service providers, found in Chapter 11.

7. DURATION
How Long Copyrights Last

Duration is the term of a copyright's existence before it falls into the public domain for free use by anyone. However, not all authors or types of work enjoy the same copyright duration. This term varies according to the creation date, type of author and copyright renewal date.

Determination of duration has changed as copyright law has been amended. The 1909 Copyright Act ("1909 Act") extended copyright duration to a 28- year term plus a renewal period of 28 years. Then the 1976 Copyright Act ("1976 Act"), as amended in 1998 by the Copyright Term Extension Act ("1998 CTEA"), streamlined copyright duration by establishing a single copyright term and devising several methods to compute duration. Under current copyright law, works of authorship fall into these main categories:

- Works created on or after January 1, 1978,
- Works created but not published or registered by January 1, 1978 (with an exception if registered by January 1, 2002),
- Works with copyrights in effect at January 1, 1978, and
- Works in the public domain.

WORKS CREATED ON OR AFTER 1.1.1978

The 1976 Copyright Act has been amended several times since its effective date of January 1, 1978, including by the CTEA and other laws conforming our law to international treaties to which the United States is a signatory. Below is a discussion of duration for all authors and works created on or after this January 1, 1978 date.

- **Individual Author.** Duration of copyrights for work of authorship created on or after January 1, 1978 by an individual author is his life plus an additional 70 years after his death.

- **Joint Authors.** If a joint work was not a work-for-hire and was registered, the duration of the work for all authors is the life of the last surviving author plus 70 years after his death.

- **Work-For-Hire.** Duration on a work-for-hire is the earlier of 95 years from first publication date or 120 years from creation date.

- **Anonymous or Pseudonymous Works.** Duration for an anonymous work or for a pseudonymous work is the earlier of 95 years from first publication date or 120 years from creation.

CREATED BUT NOT PUBLISHED OR REGISTERED BEFORE 1.1.1978

The 1976 Act grants copyright protection to works that were created but not published or registered for copyright before January 1, 1978. The duration is calculated the same as for works created after January 1, 1978, with a minimum guarantee of at least 25 years of copyright protection that could not expire before December 31, 2002. Any work in this category, which was published by December 31, 2002, received an automatic 45-year extension through December 31, 2047.

- **Individual Author.** Duration of copyrights for work of authorship created on or after January 1, 1978 by an individual author is his life plus an additional 70 years after his death.

- **Joint Authors.** If a joint work was not a work-for-hire and was registered for copyright, the duration of the work for all authors is the life of the last surviving author plus 70 years after his death.

- **Work-For-Hire, Anonymous and Pseudonymous Works.** Duration for any work-for-hire, anonymous and pseudonymous works is the earlier of 95 years from first publication date or 120 years from creation date.

- **Exception: Created before 1.1.1978 & Published Between 1.1.1978 and 12.31.2002.** Duration for works created before January 1, 1978 and published between then and December 31, 2002 extends another 45 years from 2002, to December 31, 2047.

WORKS WITH COPYRIGHTS SECURED BEFORE & IN EFFECT AT 1.1.1978

Works that were copyrighted prior to January 1, 1978 with protection still in effect as of that date are subject to the duration regulations under the 1909 Act, as modified by the 1976 Act.

- **1909 Act Works In Public Domain If Not Renewed.** Under the 1909 Act, copyright secured on the date a work was published. Copyright secured in unpublished works on the date of registration. The initial duration was 28 years from registration and if renewed timely, a renewal term of another 28 years. If copyright was not renewed, the copyright expired at the end of the first 28-year term and the work fell into the public domain.

- **1909 Act Works Renewal Extended by 1976 Act.** The 1976 Act revised the 1909 Act duration for these works whose owners had renewed their copyrights timely in the first 28-year term. The 1976 Act extended the renewal from 28 to 47 years, then the 1998 CTEA extended it another 20 years, for a total renewal term of 67 years. Currently copyright on 1909 Act works that renewed have a total duration of 95 years.

- **Automatic Extension for Works in Renewal Term.** If the owner of a 1909 Act work copyrighted it after 1922 and renewed it between 1964 and 1977, duration is a total of 95 years from the end of the year in which copyright first secured in the work.

- **Automatic Renewal & Voluntary Registration.** For a 1909 Act work copyrighted between January 1, 1964 and December 31, 1977, duration was automatically renewed for a 28-year term and a 67-year renewal term, totaling 95 years, but no formal renewal registration was required.

- **Mandatory Renewal Works.** Works originally copyrighted between January 1, 1950 and December 31, 1963 and in their first term on January 1, 1978 were required to file renewals. If renewals were filed, duration of the second term will be 67, not 28 years, for a total of 95 years from publication. If no renewal was filed, copyright expired and the work is public domain now.

WORKS IN THE PUBLIC DOMAIN AT 1.1.1978

With one limited exception, works without valid copyrights in effect as of January 1, 1978 were already in the public domain. They remain public domain works free for anyone to use, including works created and copyrighted prior to 1923 and works created after 1923 without a valid renewal as required by the 1909 Act. The exception to this legal requirement is the URAA revival of some copyrights by foreign authors that expired for failure to file renewals in compliance with the 1909 Act.

TRANSFERS OF EXCLUSIVE RIGHTS

A copyright owner may transfer, or sell and assign, one or more of his exclusive rights in his work, subject to state as well as federal laws. These different methods are described below.

1. Exclusive & Nonexclusive Transfers

When a copyright owner exclusively transfers any of the

exclusive rights to a third person, the transfer must be in writing signed by the owner of the rights or his agent.

Oral exclusive transfers are not valid. However, one or more exclusive rights may be transferred orally to a third party on a nonexclusive basis.

2. Transfers by Inheritance

A copyright is an asset that may be transferred by any legal means, including transfers at death of the copyright owner, such as a bequest in a will. If the copyright owner dies without a will, the copyright may be conveyed as an asset of personal property by law.

3. Recordation of Transfers

Copyright ownership transfers may be recorded with the USCO, but are not required for the transfer to be legal. A recorded transfer with the USCO provides legal authenticity of the transfer.

4. Termination of Prior Transfers

Under the current law, a copyright owner can terminate a prior transfer after 35 years under certain conditions. For works protected under copyright prior to 1978, current law allows termination of a transfer affected by the extension of duration to 95 years.

Table 7-A below provides various durations for copyrights in works of authorship in the United States as of certain dates. Below the Table are notes shown by the use of one or two asterisks.

TABLE 7-A
COPYRIGHT DURATION AT JANUARY 1, 2021

DATE	TYPE OF WORK	TERM STATUS
Before 1901	Unpublished Works-Made-for-Hire, Anonymous and Pseudonymous Works, or by an Author with unknown death date	Public domain * (120 yrs. from date of creation)
Before 1926	Published & copyrighted, renewed or not renewed	Public domain * (95 yrs. from date of creation)
1926 - 1964	Published & copyrighted, not renewed	Public domain *
1926 - 1964	Published, copyrighted & renewed	95 yrs. after publication
Before 1951	Unpublished work	Public domain (70 yrs. after Author's death)
Before 1978	Created, not published or registered by 1978, published 1978-2002	Renewal extension through 2047
1978 and after	Created by individual Author, published with notice	Life of the Author plus 70 yrs.
1978 and after	Created by joint Authors, published with notice	Life of the last surviving Author plus 70 yrs.
1978 and after	Created as Works-for-Hire or by Anonymous or Pseudonymous Author	Earlier of 95 yrs. from publication or 120 yrs. from creation **
After 2002	Any work created	70 yrs. after Author's death; if Work-Made-for-Hire, the earlier of 95 yrs. from publication or 120 yrs. from creation.
At any time	Works prepared by a U.S. Govt. officer or employee as part of official duties	Public domain

* Some U.S. public domain works may still be protected by copyright laws in other countries.
** If Anonymous or Pseudonymous Author's identity is later revealed in U.S. copyright records, the term is the Author's life plus 70 yrs.

PART THREE

BE YOUR OWN WOLF OF WALL STREET
Add Film Value Without Increasing the Budget

8. FAIR USE
Using Copyrighted Work (Legally)

After learning about infringement and ways to resolve infringement issues, it is important to look at defenses to infringement. These legal means are available to people who use part of a third party's copyrighted work and transform it when participating in certain limited activities.

Not every use of someone else's copyrighted work is allowed by law. A set of four factors has been established by law that helps define how to use a third party's copyrighted work legally. These concepts are discussed in further detail below.

One major legal justification for using a third party's copyrighted work is "fair use." Fair use is a legal concept that is often misunderstood by filmmakers and others who wish to have access to, and use, copyrighted works owned by others.

Fair use generally refers to the legal copying, duplicating or use of materials copyrighted by someone else for a limited purpose and which transforms the material into something new. While there are no specific rules governing what this "transformation" means, it is clear that the copyrighted work is not reproduced in its entirety. Rather, only a part of the copyrighted work is utilized in another work. This use then changes, or transforms, the original work into the new work of the person relying on such fair use defense.

A preexisting copyrighted work does not have to be published to qualify for fair use. The work may be unpublished as well. The publication of the copyrighted work has no bearing to whether or not the activity qualifies as fair use.

A number of activities qualify for fair use of another's copyrighted work, which allows the person to use the copyrighted work legally as a defense to infringement. These activities include comment or critique, reporting, education or teaching, scholarship, research and parody. They are discussed in more detail below.

On the USCO website Home Page at www.copyright.gov, note the button on the left reading, "Fair Use Index - Cases and Information." This is a link to a database of all court cases relating to fair use. The index may be searched by jurisdiction or subject matter as education/ scholarship/research, film/audiovisual, internet/ digitization, music, painting/drawing/graphic, parody/satire, review/ commentary and unpublished works. Set the search terms and from the results click on any case for a detailed summary of the case, the alleged infringement and whether or not the work was held to be fair use.

Before discussing in detail the activities that qualify for fair use, it is important to understand the considerations that determine whether such an activity is protected by fair use or not.

FAIR USE

In a general discussion of fair use, the final determination of whether or not such an activity qualifies for fair use will depend on several factors. If the copyright owner learns of the use by a third party and does not believe it is fair use, the four factors below would be considered in litigation or arbitration before determining the final decision. These factors include the following:
- The purpose and character of the use of the copyrighted work; this includes whether the use is for a commercial purpose or for nonprofit educational purposes,
- The nature of the copyrighted work,
- The amount and substantiality of the part of the work used relative to the copyrighted work as a whole, in its entirety, and
- The effect of the use of the copyrighted work on the potential market for the work, or the value of the copyrighted work.

The activities that could constitute fair use of a third party's copyrighted work without written authorization include six major categories of activities performed by third parties of existing copyrighted works. These activities relate generally to the type of employment in which the third party participates.

However, regardless of any job, the four factors above determine whether the fair use doctrine applies to the work. The categories of generally accepted fair use activities and examples in which they constitute fair use or not are:

1. Comment or Criticism

Comment, sometimes referred to as "commentary," and criticism often called "critique," both refer generally to a third party's opinion or observations about a work, although comments and criticism may be used by different people for various purposes.

For example, suppose you invite an online film blogger to attend an advance screening of your movie which she does. She then posts a review that includes some word-for-word dialogue in a few scenes from the film but she does not reveal the ending of your film.

This would be considered fair use, even though the blogger copied dialogue and scenes from your film, because it meets the four factors for fair use.

The work may be for a commercial purpose, if the blogger earns revenues from the blog. The nature of the film and your invitation to the blogger to screen it evidence your intention that you wanted her to write a blog about it. The dialogue and scene description in the blog is small compared to the entire film.

Finally, the fact that the blogger did not describe the ending did not negatively influence the market. The blog, whether good, bad or indifferent, might have generated more interest in your film and increased the potential market or value of the film.

However, what if the blogger gave away the ending, describing in great detail the final scenes? If that negatively impacted potential moviegoers' attitude to your film, fair use would not be a valid defense.

2. News Reporting

Reporters who use third-party copyrighted work participate in their activities using a variety of media -- online, television, radio, newspapers, magazines, journals, entertainment trades and more.

Suppose a reporter for your local television station stands outside the movie theatre and interviews people on camera coming out of the theatre at the end of the movie. Suppose the reporter films their moviegoers' reaction and the interviewees give details about your movie, including the ending.

For this activity to be considered fair use, the reporter must edit out any interview with a discussion of the ending, or giving too many details about your film. This could negatively influence your market because people watching the news report might not go to the theatre or buy the DVD of your film.

3. Scholarship & Education

Many people have heard of an educational "exemption" to infringement. Education and teaching fall into the category of "scholarship" for fair use, but not all copying done by students and educators meets the four-factor test for fair use.

For example, a teacher buys your DVD and screens it for her film class to discuss character development, or story structure, or any number of educational topics relating to the film. The teacher legally owns the DVD but does not have any exclusive rights associated with the copyright in the film. However, as long as she shows the film during her class without charging a fee to watch the movie, that would be considered fair use.

Now change the example and suppose the teacher buys your DVD and screens it after school, charging a $5 admission fee to anyone who wants to watch it. That would not be fair use because the teacher has infringed on your exclusive right by performing the commercial function of copying and distributing your film without your authorization and earning revenues from her infringing acts.

This is also a commercial use of your film and negative affects your market for DVD sales. Fair use would not apply to the teacher's acts.

4. Research

To qualify for fair use, research using third party copyrighted works must be done for a specific purpose. This may include research for an academic degree, such as a course-assigned paper, thesis, dissertation or other educational use. Research also includes work done for scholarly papers or journals, such as peer-reviewed journals at universities and film schools.

If a scholar chooses your film to analyze for his thesis for a Master's Degree in Film Studies and he transcribes the dialogue in the film, including the ending, does this qualify as fair use? To answer that, look at the purpose and distribution of the thesis.

Suppose the student turns in his thesis to the members of the academic committee who read the paper and keep one physical copy in the academic files of the school. The scholar is awarded his degree and keeps a copy on his computer but never publishes it in a journal or posts it online or sends it to others. This could still qualify as fair use if the commercial value of your film has not been diminished by the paper.

However, what if a committee member publishes the thesis in a journal or posts it online? That could affect sales of the film since the ending is revealed. Anyone reading the paper or the post might not be interested in seeing or buying your film. Such negative impact on your film could constitute infringement, not fair use.

5. Parody

Parody refers to a work that is a comedic or ridiculous imitation of, or take on, a third party's copyrighted work. Parody requires the taking of at least some of the copyrighted work in order to create a well-done comedic work.

An example of a parody of a film is a mockumentary film. The mockumentary can utilize parts, lines, characters, and storylines from one or more copyrighted films, told with the mockumentary's comedic style for fair use. A mockumentary of a horror film can be made as a comedy but utilizing parts of the original horror movie, like dialogue, characters, scenes, set pieces and the like. Sketch comedy television shows with skits or vignettes that give a comedic spin to other copyrighted work are other examples.

However, a remake of a copyrighted film, or a sequel to the film, would not qualify as fair use without the comedic parody as the foundation of the new work.

ATTRIBUTION

An important concept relating to fair use is "attribution," which means giving credit to the author and his work when used or referenced in a new work. Attribution is required for all uses even if relying on the fair use defense.

To give attribution to the author of a film, you may wish to choose from one of many accepted styles of formatting: These include: (i) the Chicago style (CMS) in *The Chicago Manual of Style, 16th edition,* (ii), the MLA style, Modern Language Association *MLA Handbook, 7th edition* and, (iii) the APA style, in the *APA Style: Publication Manual of the American Psychological Association.* The editions referenced are current as of this book's publication date.

An example of each type of attribution style is shown below using the following facts. A film student writes a paper on the film *My World of Jacks* by director John B. Jacks and wants to attribute the film in the paper per fair use requirements.

The motion picture is based on Jillian Barter's screenplay, produced by Jillian Barter for Satellite Studios and distributed on film by Movies Worldwide, Inc. in Atlanta, Georgia beginning January 15, 2001. The attribution can be one of the following:

- **Chicago (CMS) Format:** Person/persons responsible for the content Last Name, First. *Film Title*. Medium. Directed by First Name Last Name. Distributor City: Distributor, Year of Release.
  Citation: Barter, Jillian. *My World of Jacks*. Film. Directed by John B. Jacks. Atlanta: Movies Worldwide, Inc., 2001.

- **MLA Format:** *Film title*. Dir. First Name Last Name. Distributor, Year of Release. Medium.
  Citation: *My World of Jacks.* Dir. John B. Jacks. Movies Worldwide, Inc., 2001. Film.

- **APA Format:** Last name, first initial (Producer), & Last name, first initial (Director). (Release Year). *Title of motion picture* [Motion Picture]. Country of Origin: Studio.
  Citation: Barter, J. (Producer), & Jacks, J. (Director). (2011). *My World of Jacks* [Motion Picture]. USA: Satellite Studios.

As seen above, each style is slightly different from the other two. Sometimes a specific style is required by particular educational institution or employer. Alternatively, the person citing the work selects the style he prefers.

It is important to acknowledge authors of copyrighted works when using those works, but especially when a free license is available and requires such attribution. Failure to do so could result in penalties and the cancellation of the license, depending on the licensing agreement.

9. PUBLIC DOMAIN

Free Public Domain Content vs. Free or Fee-Based Licensed Content

Works in the public domain and works licensed in the "commons" are often misunderstood. You know that duration of a copyright work expires after a period of time based on certain conditions, including the type of author and whether the work was published or unpublished.

Published works whose copyrights have expired are considered to be works in the public domain and are absolutely free for use by anyone. Public domain works can be accessed, copied or revised for personal or commercial use. A valuable source of public domain works, including films, videos and other works, is the U.S. Government.

Additional works accessible to the public, but subject to licensing restrictions are "open source" works, whose owners have voluntarily allowed the use of their copyrighted works. These works, often referred to as being in the "commons" are available to the public for certain uses depending on the licenses of the owners. Such open source works may have restrictions, including fees for commercial or other uses. Several sources of these works include Project Gutenberg, Project Gutenberg affiliates, Creative Commons and MIT.

Thousands of public domain and open source works are available through many sources, particularly online. Some are free for personal, non-commercial use and some require a sharing license of any work used. Others require license and a fee for commercial use. It is important to read the terms and conditions for open source works and verify any responsibility for royalty payments or other fees often due when these otherwise free works are commercialized.

A filmmaker can utilize public domain content in a film to reduce his budget by the projected cost of content acquisition, or to enrich his film with this content without any investment.

Filmmakers can also create their own derivative works of public domain works without paying licensing fees. From public domain works, filmmakers can gain invaluable inspiration and stories that can eventually become movies. Examples of films adapted from public domain content include those based on works by Shakespeare, such as "Macbeth" and "Romeo and Juliet" and public domain fairy tales such as "Cinderella" and "Snow White."

Access to public domain and open source works is valuable to a filmmaker. A primary public domain source is the U.S. Government.

U.S. GOVERNMENT PUBLIC DOMAIN WORKS

Copyright protection is not available for any work of the United States Government made by an employee in the scope of his employment. These works are in the public domain. You can freely use these works, which include films, videos, audio recordings, documents, and other works created by Government employees. However, the U.S. Government may accept and hold copyrights to works transferred to it by a bequest in a will, an assignment or other transfers.

These copyrighted works are not in the public domain and may not be used freely without verifying restrictions of the transferred work. Some sites providing free access to U.S. Government content for anyone from filmmakers to educators are discussed below.

1. Library of Congress & Prelinger Archives

The Library of Congress in Washington, D.C., is the largest library in the world and holds archives and collections of copyrighted work as well as being the official depository library for all works registered for copyright. Their website is www.loc.gov, which provides links to sites that offer free access to U.S. Government films, videos, and documents.

The Library of Congress acquired the Prelinger Archives of over 11,000 digitized film and videotape titles, industrial films and historically significant home movies not found elsewhere. Many are in the public domain and Getty Images issues licenses for the films, which are a valuable resource for period footage and education research.

2. FEDFLIX, Public.Resource.org, Internet Archive

Public.Resource.Org is a nonprofit 501(c)(3) corporation that runs the website, www.Public.Resource.org. This site provides online access to government information in the public domain, including high-resolution videos, archives of other U.S. government databases and C-Span videos, among other resources. The corporation and the National Technical Information Service Library compiled and uploaded U.S. government videotapes and clips to YouTube, the Internet Archive and government servers.

The site also provides access to FEDFLIX, which provides U.S. government films free for all uses. Such content can be a valuable resource for filmmakers, such as in opening or title sequences, for stock footage, or for other uses.

Films can be searched by topic, date, title and other means. A recent search yielded over 8,700 U.S. Government films including, "Liberation of Rome," "Moonwalk One," "Bailout Congressional Hearings," "The Story of Hoover Dam" and "China." See http://archive.org/details/FedFlix.

Examples of subjects include:
- Declassified Security Council, CIA films,
- U.S. Congressional hearings,
- U.S. history, and
- Air Force, Army, Coast Guard, Marine Corps and Navy.

3. FEDLINK

The Federal Library and Information Network (FEDLINK) is an organization of federal agencies that work to maximize the resources of federal libraries and information centers and make them available to the public, usually for personal or educational purposes. FEDLINK provides a forum for discussion, which may be useful to filmmakers, film students and educators. From an educational, scholarship and research fair use perspective, FEDLINK provides access to valuable information and links. Generally, duplication rates apply to requests for copies of videos, photographs and other records. The website is www.loc.gov/flicc.

COMMONS CONTENT

Many mistakenly belief that anything on the Internet, including posts on social media platforms, can be used freely. However, since much of that work is copyrighted, use is an infringement. However, a substantial amount of open source content is available for use by anyone. Much open source content is free for private use, but subject to a licensing fee for commercial use. However, students, researchers, educators and others may apply fair use and access even more content.

Several open source commons licenses are often used, such as the Creative Commons license, the MIT License for open source educational courses, and others. However, not all content on these sites are for all uses. To determine the exclusive rights of copyright that are made available to the general public, review the license terms and conditions.

A number of licenses are offered on such sites. Some licenses offer free content for personal or education use, while others require licenses for commercial use. When searching sites for content for a film, it is crucial to verify if the work is in the public domain or if the owner's license agreement allows such commercial use.

1. Project Gutenberg

Filmmakers can get inspiration from works of authorship of others, especially books. Consider all the books, plays, fairy tales, stories and other works that have been in the public domain for sometimes centuries that have been made into films.

The Project Gutenberg ("Project Gutenberg") is a non-profit 501(c)3 non-profit corporation that as of the date of publication of this book, offers over 50,000 digital books online at its website, www.gutenberg.org. Many works are in English, but also are available in numerous foreign languages including French, German, Italian and Portuguese, to name a few.

Project Gutenberg requires users of its site to accept the site licensing agreement that incorporates user rights, limited warranties and the use of the Project Gutenberg trademark. The license also covers two different categories of texts.

The first licensing category is for books that are not protected by U.S. copyright laws, primarily due to the expiration of the copyright duration on the works. The second category is for copyrighted books for which the owners of the copyrights have given Project Gutenberg the right to distribute them on the website.

Websites for Project Gutenberg and its affiliates are available in the Free Materials section in the back of the book. Many of these sites offer free content, some have thousands of free titles, and others provide content accessibility on mobile devices.

2. Creative Commons

In addition to free content in the public domain and certain open source works, a unique opportunity exists for filmmakers to access and use third-party copyrighted content through Creative Commons. Creative Commons is a nonprofit organization that is facilitates the sharing of copyrighted works with others legally and allows third parties to use copyrighted work on the site. Whether the work is free depends on the license, which generally is subject to the type of use.

In essence, this legal sharing site provides a clearinghouse for copyright owners to select the conditions they choose to share their work with the public. The website for this association is www.creativecommons.org.

Copyright owners who contribute their works to Creative Commons do so pursuant to a license of their choice. Currently, six different licenses are offered, listed below in the order of the least restrictive to the most onerous:

- A license that allows third parties to use the work in a new work for all purposes, even commercial, if the third party gives credit, or "attribution," for the original creator's work.

- A license that allows the same as above and additionally requires the third party to license the new work under the same terms.

- A license that allows the work to be distributed in its entirety and without changing anything, for commercial and non-commercial purposes attributing the original creator.

- A license that allows others to use the work for non-commercial use, with attribution to the original creator.

- A license that allows others to use the work in a new work for non-commercial purposes, with attribution to the original creator and a license of the new work under the same terms.

- A license that allows others to download and share the work with others, attributing the original creator; however, no changes may be made to the original work and no commercial uses are permitted.

Members of the general public have the right to access and use the work in accordance with the terms of the particular license determined by the actual copyright holder at the time of donation.

In viewing the site, suppose a filmmaker sees a photograph that expresses the essence of his film. He wishes to use it for the poster of his movie, to promote it, sell posters on a crowdfunding site or for other commercial use. Whether or not the filmmaker could use this photograph without payment of a fee will depend on the license associated with the photo. If the photographer donated the photo to Creative Commons under a free license, but requires attribution, the filmmaker could utilize it by giving credit to the photographer.

CONTRIBUTE WORK TO THE COMMONS

Copyright owners who want to give the public access to their work can donate their work into the "commons" independently or with an organization. The filmmaker decides on the type of license for his film, which may be free for all uses, or subject to fee-based licensing for other uses. By doing so, he may voluntarily reduce his legal copyright duration although may still license the work for compensation.

COPYRIGHT PROTECTION ASSOCIATIONS

In the United States, several non-profit associations exist that promote policies or awareness and education about copyright. One such entity is the Copyright Alliance, whose membership includes major entertainment industry and other organizations include those in film, television, music, publishing, art, photography, acting, directing and other areas. Its website is www.copyrightalliance.org.

Another organization is The Copyright Society of the USA, a nonprofit established in 1953 that focuses on education and awareness of copyright law. It holds meetings each year and publishes *The Journal of the Copyright Society of the USA.* Its website is found at www.csusa.org. The References section provides contact information for these and other associations.

10. DESIGN ASSETS
Film-Related Designs vs. VARA Works

A filmmaker builds wealth in the entertainment industry through his Intellectual Property. Yet many filmmakers are unaware of the numerous film-related designs created for a film that are assets.

These design assets can be copyrighted to build wealth. Such works include film posters, on-set art, photographs and other works made for the film by designers on work-for-hire agreements. In addition, fictional characters created for a film that are distinctive and integral to the story, not merely stereotypes, can be copyrighted as well.

These film-related design assets are copyrightable as works of visual art on Form VA, if visually artistic form. Copyrighted fictional characters can be licensed for merchandising in a myriad of ways, including but not limited to, clothing, toys, games, video games, linens, theme parks, dishes and glassware, jewelry, food products, and much more. The filmmaker can, and should, registered these designs, for copyright and exploit their exclusive rights as much as possible.

However, the filmmaker should be aware of certain rights granted by the Visual Artists Rights Act of 1990 ("VARA") to authors of fine arts and exhibition photographs. VARA is the first copyright legislation in the United States to grant "moral rights" to some authors of works of the visual art, following the model suggested in the Berne Convention for the Protection of Literary and Artistic Works, discussed in Chapter 12.

These moral rights guarantee certain authors the right to claim or disclaim authorship in a work, additional rights to prevent distortion, mutilation or modification of a work and in some instances the right to prevent a work incorporated into a building from being destroyed.

Moral rights are derived from the French concept of "droit moral" that originated for publishers in the mid-1500's and for authors in the following century to protect the essence of the author embodied in the work and protecting his honor. A partial list of the types of designs filmmakers can and cannot copyright are listed below. A discussion follows on VARA works and the rights and remedies of VARA authors, even after selling their exclusive rights and fine art work to a third party.

COPYRIGHTABLE DESIGNS

If a work of visual art created for a film is not a work of stature such as a painting by a leading artist, or the visual work is a work-for-hire, that work can be registered and protected under U.S. copyright law. To be copyrightable, the design must be original or make a useful article more attractive or more distinctive to the public that uses or purchases such an article, with some creativity and fixed in a tangible form.

Some examples of copyrightable designs for a filmmaker whose designers are on work-for-hire agreements include:
- A storyboard,
- Distinctive fictional characters in the film,
- A film poster, and the designs and photos in a film poster,
- A tattoo designed for a cast member,
- Art painted for use on a film set, and
- A distinctive horror mask made for a film.

A filmmaker may register these works of visual art for copyright and then exploit the exclusive rights to the works. The filmmaker owns the copyright and exclusive rights on these designs. They do not qualify as a VARA visual work of art being a work-for-hire and not fine art.

NON-PROTECTED DESIGNS

A design is not protected by copyright that is:
- Not original,
- Commonplace, such as a geometric form, symbol, emblem, motif or another shape, pattern or configuration which has become common or ordinary,

- Insignificantly different from the common designs above or only with different elements used commonly in relevant trades,
- Designed only by a useful function of the item that contains it, or
- Contained or embodied in a useful article made public in the U.S. or abroad more than two years before registration.

SPECIAL RIGHTS FOR VISUAL WORKS AUTHORS

A filmmaker should understand what rights are granted to authors of works of fine visual art pursuant to the Visual Artists Rights Act. This information is important to filmmakers in the event they acquire a work of visual art protected by this copyright law or wish to use such a work in a film.

These VARA rights include the rights of attribution and integrity below.

1. Right of Attribution (VARA)

The right of attribution under VARA of an author of a VARA-protected work is independent of the exclusive rights. Attribution for an author is receiving credit for his work. VARA attribution is expanded to include the following rights:

- To claim authorship of the work,

- To prevent the use of his name as the author of any work of visual art he did not create,

- To prevent the use of his name as the author of the work of visual art if it is distorted, mutilated, or otherwise modified that would be prejudicial to his honor or reputation, and

- To prevent any intention modification that would be prejudicial to his reputation or honor.

The author of the work of visual arts protected by VARA owns these rights, even if someone else owns the work. If a filmmaker hires a mask designer to create unusual horror masks for a film on a work-for-hire agreement, the filmmaker would own the exclusive copyright rights to the masks and the designer has no VARA rights.

However, if a famous painter creates a mask that the filmmaker later buys and intentionally smashes or spatters with green paint, whether used in the film or not, the filmmaker has violated the painter's right of attribution. If two famous painters jointly create the mask, they are co-owners of the right of attribution.

The author of a work of visual art also has the right of integrity more fully explained below.

2. Right of Integrity (VARA)

The right of integrity held by the creator of a visual work is independent of the exclusive rights of the owner of the copyright in and to the visual work. Subject to certain limitations, including when a building is destroyed, this right prohibits:

- Intentional distortion, mutilation or other modification of the work that would be prejudicial to the author's reputation or honor,

- Destruction of a work of recognized stature and any intentional or grossly negligent destruction of the work, and

- Destruction of a work of recognized stature and any intentional or grossly negligent destruction of that work.

VARA is an exception to the copyright first sale doctrine in that the owner, who is not the author, of a work is subject to the VARA rights of attribution and integrity during the author's lifetime.

If a work of visual art is modified over time by the inherent nature of the materials, restoration of a damaged work or similar situations, such acts do not violate the author's VARA rights.

WORKS COVERED & NOT COVERED BY VARA

VARA rights extend only to limited categories of works of visual art classified as fine art and are single copies or limited editions of up to two hundred signed and numbered copies of each of these works:
- Sculptures,
- Paintings,
- Drawings,
- Prints, and
- Still photographs produced for exhibition.

Many works are excluded from VARA coverage, including:
- Motion pictures or other audiovisual works,
- Work-for-hire,
- Maps, globes or charts,
- Posters,
- Technical drawings, diagrams, models,
- Applied art,
- Books, magazines, newspapers, periodicals, data bases, electronic information services, electronic publications or similar publications,
- Merchandising items or advertising or any promotional, descriptive, covering or packaging materials or container, or
- Other item not subject to general copyright protection.

DURATION

VARA was enacted in 1990 with an effective date of June 1, 1991 and set forth terms of duration under two sets of ownership circumstances:

- Duration for VARA works created on or after the effective date or for works created before that date but whose ownership rights were not transferred until after the effective date, VARA rights last for the life of the author, and

- Works created prior to the VARA effective date of June 1, 1991 are protected for the same term as a copyrighted work, which is currently the life of the author plus 70 years.

VARA TRANSFER OF OWNERSHIP & WAIVER

If an author of a work of visual art protected by VARA transfers the ownership of the copyright or any of the exclusive rights in the work, such transfer is not a waiver of any VARA rights unless otherwise specified in a writing signed by the author. The written agreement must specify the work and the uses to which the waiver applies. No other rights granted pursuant to VARA are waived by such a written agreement.

VARA JOINT WORKS

Duration for joint works of visual art protected by VARA and created by two or more authors lasts for the life of the last surviving author. If one joint author waives any of the VARA rights for the joint work, he waives all rights for all joint authors.

REMEDIES

Being a part of U.S. copyright law, VARA provides the same remedies for violation as for copyright infringement, with the added requirement of valuing the violation's effect on the reputation and standing of the artist. This condition may require the opinion of an expert and could be costly. Remedies for copyright infringement found in Chapter 6 are discussed in detail.

If a person alters or modifies a VARA protected work, the resulting work could be considered a derivative work subject to an infringement claim under copyright law. If the person tries to claim that he is the owner of a work protected by VARA, such claim may violate the author's right of publicity, as discussed in Chapter 15.

PART FOUR

✱

DIGITAL WAR OF THE WORLDS
The Copyright Digital Age & Beyond

11. DMCA

The Long Arm of the Law Against Digital Piracy

As discussed in Chapter 4, copyright law has changed a number of times since its inception in the United States Constitution. For filmmakers, one of the most significant legal changes to copyright law is the Digital Millennium Copyright Act of 1998 ("DMCA").

The DMCA was enacted to integrate into U.S. law the obligations of two World Intellectual Property Organization (WIPO) treaties to which the United States is a signatory. These obligations require legal prohibitions against circumventing technological means used by copyright owners to protect their works, and against removing or altering copyright management information. In the DMCA, Congress also facilitated the development of electronic commerce and the distribution of digital works by creating anti-piracy provisions.

DMCA - ANTI-PIRACY LAW

A major issue for filmmakers, is unauthorized use of copyrighted works by posts, uploads, peer-to-peer sharing and other online infringement. The DMCA also addresses remedies for copyright owners who discover infringing acts on their works, including severe penalties for Infringers. This legislation also addresses responsibilities of service providers, including limitations on liability and safe harbors.

Additionally, the first sale doctrine is not applied to digital works as it is for physical copies, since digital copying and transfers impact both the exclusive rights of distribution and copying or reproduction.

The DMCA incorporates five different titles, of which three are relevant to filmmakers. The titles and their major points are below:

- **Title I:** The WIPO Copyright and Performances and Phonograms Treaties Implementation Act of 1998 provides the following:
    - Implementation of the WIPO Copyright Treaty and the WIPO Performances and Phonograms Treaty to protect pre-existing foreign works that have not fallen into the public domain in the relevant country of origin,
    - Exemption for foreign works from registration with the U.S. Copyright Office before filing an infringement suit,
    - Prohibition against making or selling devices to circumvent measures such as Digital Rights Management ("DRM") to protect unauthorized access to or unauthorized copying (and other exclusive rights such as distribution and public performance) of copyrighted works, with fair use exceptions,
    - Prohibition against the removal or alteration of electronic Copyright Management Information ("CMI"), and
    - Criminal penalties for violation, ranging from $500,000 and five years in prison for the first offense up to $1 million and 10 years in prison for the second or later offenses.

- **Title II:** The Online Copyright Infringement Liability Limitation Act provides the following:
    - Liability limits for online service providers for: (i) transitory communications as a data conduit from one point to another at a user's request, (ii) system caching to retain temporary copies online in data transmission, (iii) storage of information at direction of users, and (iv) information location tools such as hyperlinks, search engines and such,
    - Requirement that online service providers designate an agent to receive notice of infringement claims.

- **Title IV:** Provides additional provisions including those for:
    - Copyright Act infringement exceptions for libraries and ephemeral recordings of music for later broadcast,
    - "Webcasting" sound recordings, and

- Application of collective bargaining agreements to motion picture copyright transfers.

Additional details of the Digital Millennium Copyright Act important to filmmakers and other copyright owners follow.

DRM AND CMI - DIGITAL RIGHTS MANAGEMENT & COPYRIGHT MANAGEMENT INFORMATION

As seen in Title I of the DMCA, it is illegal to make or sell devices that circumvent a copyright owner's measures to prevent access or unauthorized infringement on the exclusive rights of his work.

Digital Rights Management ("DRM") is technology that limits access to copying, often used to protect against duplication of motion pictures. The DMCA makes illegal any DRM circumvention, even without copying the work.

Copyright Management Information ("CMI") is electronic or other information in a copyrighted work identifying the type of work and the owner. It is illegal under the DMCA to alter or remove such CMI.

CMI in a motion picture or other audiovisual work usually includes the name and other identifying information about the key creative talent credited in the film, such as the writer, director or talent.

DIGITAL COPYRIGHT INFRINGEMENT

Online copyright infringement in today's digital society is an ever-growing issue. Under the DMCA, copyright owners who discover unauthorized digital copies of their works online now have the ability to have such copies taken down or to have unauthorized access to their works blocked by online service providers.

The DMCA procedure to remove infringing copies from a service provider network or system is called a "notice-and-takedown." This remedy, as well as counter-actions that may be taken by alleged infringers is discussed below. Limitations on liability of service providers are also explained.

1. Service Provider Definition

For all purposes except merely as a conduit of data, the DMCA defines "service provider" as:

"a provider of online services or network access, or the operator of facilities therefor, including an entity offering the transmission, routing, or providing of connections for digital online communications, between or among points specified by a user, of material of the user's choosing, without modification to the content of the material as sent or received."

2. Service Provider Liability Limitations

Liability for infringement by a service provider is limited if it:
- Does not have actual knowledge of the infringement,
- Is not aware of facts or circumstances from which the infringing act is apparent, or
- Upon gaining such knowledge or awareness of the infringement, responds expeditiously to block access to the material or take it down.

Below is the site to locate the agent for a service provider in order to provide notification of infringement on the provider's network or system.

3. Service Provider Agents for Infringement Notice

The USCO maintains a list on its website of online service provider agents who are authorized to receive infringement claims. The site is www.copyright.gov/onlinesp/list/a_agents.htm.

Select the provider on whose network or system the infringing act or activities occur and send notification of the infringement according to the notice-and-take-down procedure described below.

4. Notice-and-Takedown Procedure for Owners

The DMCA provides a remedy for copyright owners to prevent online access to unauthorized copies of the owners' works. The process to remove the infringing copy from the Internet is a procedure known as "notice-and-takedown."

Under this process, the copyright owner completes a written notice under penalty of perjury and submits it with a listing of specified elements to the service provider's designated agent. The agent list is on the USCO website as noted above.

The service provider must promptly comply with this takedown notice and remove or disable access to the material. If the provider receives a counter-notification from the subscriber that uploaded or sent the material through the system, the provider must put back, or allow access to, the material within ten to fourteen days unless the provider receives notice of a lawsuit against the subscriber.

The copyright owner must comply with all DMCA requirements or the notification will not be utilized to determine the service provider's knowledge and the extent of its liability. The DMCA requires a written communication to the designated agent of the service provider with information about the copyrighted work or works claimed to be the subject of infringing activity, as follows:

- A physical or electronic signature of the owner or agent of the owner claiming the infringement,

- Identification of the copyrighted work or a list of multiple works on one online site,

- Identification of the material to be removed or access to be disabled, with reasonably sufficient information to allow the service provider to locate it,

- Reasonably sufficient information to allow the service provider to contact the complaining party, such as address, phone number, and if available, electronic mail address,

- Statement that the owner has a good faith belief that use of the work in the manner complained of is not authorized by the copyright owner, his agent or the law,

- Statement that the information in the takedown notification is accurate and that the owner declares, under penalty of perjury, that he is the owner or is authorized to act on behalf of the owner of an exclusive right of copyright in the work that is allegedly infringed.

5. Counter Response Procedure for Subscribers

The person who uploads or sends the copyrighted material using a service provider's network or system is called the "subscriber." Subscribers are provided an opportunity to send a counter response to any notice and takedown from copyright owners for the material the subscriber put on the provider's network. The subscriber must file a counter notification under penalty of perjury complying with DMCA requirements, including that the material was removed or disabled through mistake or misidentification.

6. Service Provider Response and Liability Limitations

When the service provider receives proper notification of infringing material on its network or system and promptly removes or blocks access to the material, the provider is not liable for monetary penalties to the notifying party. The provider is also protected from liability for subscriber claims for the provider's takedown of the subscriber's material. For protection, the service provider must promptly notify the uploading subscriber that the provider has removed or disabled access to the material.

If the subscriber sends a counter notification and the copyright owner does not file a lawsuit for a court order such as an injunction against the subscriber, the service provider is required to re-post the material to the site within ten to fourteen business days.

7. Penalties for Improper Notices

The DMCA establishes penalties for any person who knowingly makes a material misrepresentation in a takedown notice or counter notice that the online material is infringing, or that it was removed or blocked by mistake or misidentification.

These penalties include all damages incurred by the subscriber, copyright owner, owner's licensee or the service provider. These damages include costs and reasonable attorney's fees.

MOTION PICTURE RIGHTS TRANSFERS

In accordance with Title IV of the DMCA, a transfer of copyright ownership in the rights of a motion picture on or after the DMCA effective date is subject to additional requirements under the DMCA, unless the transfer is limited to the right to perform publicly.

1. Collective Bargaining

If a motion picture was produced subject to collective bargaining agreements such as Guild or union agreements, the new copyright owner in the film is required to assume all contractual obligations in such collective bargaining agreements as of the time of the transfers.

The transferor is responsible to notify the transferee of such applicable collective bargaining obligations prior to signature of the transfer agreement. For failure to notify, the transferor is liable to the transferee for the transferee's damages.

2. Public Performance Exclusion

If the transfer of rights to a motion picture is for the right to perform the work publicly, the transferee is exempt from collective bargaining obligations. Public performances include rights transfers to a broadcast station, cable system, programmer or other transferee acting as an exhibitor of the film directly on its own network, system, service or station, or by initiating a transmission carried by another such transferee. This exclusion does not apply if the transferee is also a producer or distributor of the motion picture.

3. Disputes & Claims

Disputes relating to these transfers of motion picture rights are resolved by litigation in a United States District Court. The court has discretion to order one party to pay all the costs, including reasonable attorney's fees to the winning party.

A transferee may choose to defer performance required under the collective bargaining agreement if there is a bona fide dispute between a Guild or union and a prior transferor until resolution of such dispute. However, such deferral does not defer any of the guild or union claims under the relevant agreement.

DMCA EFFECTIVE DATES

Most DMCA provisions are effective as of the DMCA enactment date, October 28, 1998. However, Title I provisions of the new WIPO treaties take effect when such treaties come into force. The prohibition on circumventing access control measures takes effect on October 28, 2000. The DMCA has strengthened rights and remedies of copyright owners whose works are infringed online, set penalties for infringers, defined liability for service providers and conformed U.S. copyright law to WIPO treaties. In Chapter 12, these and other international agreements are discussed.

PART FIVE

✽

IT'S A SMALL, SMALL, SMALL, SMALL WORLD
International Copyright Agreements, Issues & Solutions

12. INTERNATIONAL TREATIES
Protect Your Film Globally Without Leaving the USA

This Chapter discusses the international copyright agreements that the United States has executed with other nations. These agreements are sometimes referred to as conventions or treaties, which mean agreements between nations.

Global efforts have been undertaken by the United States and other nations through intellectual property agreements to standardize intellectual property protections in signatory countries. These protections to respect and protect intellectual property rights of works of their own citizens and the citizens of other signatory countries are implemented into each country's national laws.

Many filmmakers have the opportunity to screen, distribute or sell their film internationally. International film distribution can be accomplished in many ways, including through a sales agent, international distributors, participation in international film festivals and digital uploads, among other means. The idea of distributing a film globally is exciting, although opportunities raise many questions. How can the copyright on a film be protected in countries outside the United States? Do other nations respect a U.S. film copyright in their respective countries? If so, what is the duration of the copyright protection and under what conditions? Which countries should a filmmaker avoid when distributing his film internationally?

The concept of an "international copyright" providing instant protection from infringement of an author's works around the globe does not exist. Copyright protection in countries throughout the world depends on the particular laws of those nations, which vary from one country to the next. Works copyrighted in one country have been vulnerable to infringement in another country, particularly through digital means as shown in Chapter 11.

Although an international copyright is non-existent, filmmakers and other copyright owners who have created their works of authorship in the United States, whether registered or not, have copyright protection of their works in certain foreign countries. Through international treaties, a work created and protected by copyright law in the United States may be also protected in the treaty member countries to the same extent as the works of citizens of those countries.

These agreements are beneficial to authors because they offer reciprocal protection to citizens of one country in the other countries that have signed the agreements. These international agreements provide that the United States must honor the copyrights of works of citizens of signatory countries, and likewise, that those nations honor American citizens' copyrights.

However, not every country has signed every agreement. In fact, many nations have not signed any agreements at all protecting copyright or other IP rights of their citizens or the citizens of other nations. Many countries do not have laws protecting copyright or if laws do exist, the nations may not enforce them. As a result, many works protected by the U.S. or signatory countries have no protection at all in the non-signatory nations.

A valuable benefit to copyright holders of works registered in the United States is that any such copyright-related international treaty, act, protocol or other agreement to which the United States is a party grants American citizens the same copyright protection in those signatory countries as they grant their own citizens.

It is true that some nations may have different copyright protection duration or other terms than the United States offers. However, whatever rights and protections the signatory nation grants to its own citizens are granted to U.S. citizens with copyrights registered in this country. This procedure thus protects a U.S. filmmaker's motion picture in signatory countries without ever leaving home.

INTERNATIONAL AGREEMENTS

The world continues to shrink as technology speeds communication and works are made and distributed around the globe and whose authors seek copyright protection. Some of the most important international intellectual property agreements to which the United States is a signatory, and the copyright protections offered to works by authors in the United States and other countries, are discussed below.

1. Berne Convention of 1886 and the Berne Convention Implementation Act of 1988

The Berne Convention for the Protection of Literary and Artistic Works (the "Berne Convention") was initially signed at Berne, Switzerland, on September 9, 1886 by many countries and thereafter revised numerous times. Revision locations and dates include Paris (1896), Berlin (1908), Berne (1914), Rome (1928), Brussels (1948), Stockholm (1967) and Paris (1971), with additional amendments thereafter in 1979.

During this process, the United States was not a signatory, resisting because of certain duration requirements, among other Convention obligations. However, the United States enacted the Berne Convention Implementation Act of 1988 ("Implementation Act") which became effective March 1, 1989. This Implementation Act conformed U.S. law to the requirements of the Berne Convention and the United States became a signatory, joining over 170 countries and the Holy See of Rome.

The Berne Convention addresses the IP protection of works and rights of their authors. The Convention as amended requires, among other conditions, that signatory countries grant at a minimum:

- **Independence of protection**: A grant of the same protection to foreign works as the country grants authors of domestic works, even if the foreign works are not protected by copyright in the country of origin,

- **National treatment**: Providing the same level of copyright protection to literary and artistic works by authors from signatory countries as the country grants its authors, and

- **Automatic protection**: Copyright protection to unpublished works immediately upon creation of the work without requiring any formality, including registration.

The Berne Convention was the forerunner of copyright law as we know it in the United States today. Among other progressive ideas in it declared that copyright exists at the moment a work is fixed and eliminated formal registration to protect the copyright in the work. It also requires members to grant copyright protection of a work for a minimum duration of the life of the author plus fifty years.

Although the member countries respect the Berne Convention and do not require registration for a work to receive copyright protection, most countries do offer a method of formal registration of a copyright. This formality, while optional for protection, may still be required for other benefits. In the United States, registration is required to qualify for statutory damages and attorney's fees for infringement of a work, as discussed in Chapter 6.

A "Berne Convention Work" is an original work of authorship created under the original Berne Convention of 1888, but prior to March 1, 1989, the date of the Implementation Act when the United States adhered to the Berne Convention terms and eliminated the use of a copyright notice for a "Berne Convention Work."

2. General Agreement on Tariffs and Trade (GATT)

The General Agreement on Tariffs and Trade ("GATT") is an international treaty signed by the United States and other nations, which, among other provisions, requires the signatory countries to comply with the Berne Convention copyright protections. The GATT treaty also provides for the registration of any works:

- In which the U.S. copyright was restored according to the 1994 Uruguay Round Agreements Act ("URAA"),

- First published in the United States or in a foreign nation that, on the date of first publication, is a treaty member, or

- Published in the United States or a treaty member within 30 days after publication in a foreign nation that is not a treaty party shall be considered to be first published in the United States or such treaty party, as the case may be, or

- Of foreign origin in the public domain in the United States prior to 1996 and its copyright was restored under the Uruguay Round Agreements Act ("URAA").

In the United States, use Form GATT to register with the USCO any restored single work or a series of works published under a single title in multiple episodes, installments, or issues in a calendar year.

GATT also restores copyright protection for certain foreign works that have lost copyright in the United States for these reasons:

- Failure to comply with certain "formalities" of United States law, like publication without a notice prior to March 1, 1989,

- Failure to renew a work copyrighted pursuant to prior law within the required time limit for that work,

- Lack of subject matter protection for sound recordings fixed before February 15, 1972, or

- Lack of national eligibility.

3. World Intellectual Property Organization (WIPO) Internet Treaties

The World Intellectual Property Organization ("WIPO") is a self-funding agency of the United Nations, headquartered in Geneva,

Switzerland. WIPO is a forum for intellectual property services, policy, information and cooperation among its members totaling 188 at present. WIPO administers the WIPO Copyright Treaty of 1996 ("WCT") and the WIPO Performances and Phonograms Treaty of 1996, collectively referred to as the "WIPO Internet Treaties."

These Treaties require signatory countries to protect preexisting works from other WIPO member countries that are not in the public domain in the country of origin. Protection must be no less favorable than what the member country grants to its citizens.

WCT members must also grant copyright protection to computer programs and databases, and prohibit circumventing technologies to prevent copyright and distribution of copyrighted works, such as encryption or rights management information.

WIPO offers a website entitled WIPO Lex, a database of the international intellectual property legislation and treaties of member countries at www.wipo.int/wipolex/en/ that also provides information about the IP laws of each such country.

4. Uruguay Round Agreements Act of 1994 (URAA)

The United States is also a party to the Uruguay Round Agreements Act ("URAA") which restored copyrights in certain foreign works that were originally published in the United States without a formal notice of copyright and fell into the public domain in the U.S. as provided in the GATT treaty.

5. WTO Agreement on Trade-Related Aspects of Intellectual Property Rights (TRIPs)

The Agreement on Trade-Related Aspects of Intellectual Property, often referred to as "TRIPS," is an international treaty administered by World Trade Organization ("WTO") protecting intellectual property in international trade. The TRIPS treaty was agreed to by WTO members during the URAA in 1994.

This treaty provides that WTO member states grant copyright rights to content producers, performers, producers of sound recordings and broadcasting organizations and others. It also stipulates procedures for enforcement and resolution of disputes between the signatories. Additionally, any WTO members who are not party to the Berne Convention must also grant the same rights of "Independence of Protection," "National Treatment" and "Automatic Protection" of copyright. TRIPS also implemented an exclusive right of rental for audiovisual works under certain conditions.

Duration of copyright protection for a work pursuant to the TRIPS Agreement, if calculated on any basis other than a natural person's life, must be at least 50 years from the date of the first authorized publication or creation of the work except photographic or applied art works.

6. Universal Copyright Convention

This international agreement signed in Geneva, Switzerland in 1952 is administered by the United Nations Educational, Scientific, and Cultural Organization ("UNESCO"). The treaty was developed by UNESCO, partly in response to some countries' objections to the Berne Convention requirements. This agreement is not as important as it once was, since nearly all signatories are WTO members, conforming to the TRIPS agreement.

WORKS BY FOREIGN AUTHORS

An original work of authorship that meets all the criteria for copyright in the United States may be registered by a foreign author. Whether a work of foreign origin created outside the United States may be registered in the United States depends on the law and registration requirements of the nation. Unpublished works by foreign or U.S. citizens are all protected under copyright law in the United States.

Per certain international agreements, works of authorship that are first published in the United States or in signatory countries are also protected and may be registered for copyright here, pursuant to the terms of the agreements. The benefits are numerous to U.S. copyright holders by virtue of these international agreements.

WORLD TRADE ORGANIZATION (WTO)

The World Trade Organization ("WTO") is an association of governments from throughout the world that negotiate matters of international commerce and resolve trade disputes among themselves. WTO members must comply with the Berne Convention substantive law provisions even if such members are not signatories to the Convention except that WTO members not signatories are not required to adhere to the moral rights provisions of the Convention.

WATCH LISTS AND NOTORIOUS MARKETS

The United States Trade Representative monitors foreign IP activity and prepares Watch Lists of countries with insufficient IP protection and of Notorious Markets, online and physical, that distribute pirated copyrighted work. In April 2016 the *U.S. Special 301 Report* listed 24 countries on the "Priority Watch List" and 10 nations on the "Watch List." Over 50 markets are on the "Notorious Market" list, in References in the back of the book.

NON-TREATY COUNTRIES

Many nations are not signatories to any IP treaties with the United States and do not protect U.S. copyrighted works. Research each country of interest to verify IP legislation for U.S. copyrighted works.

PART SIX

✱

There's No Crying in Copyrights!
Step-by-Step Copyright Registration to DIY Right Every Time

13. REGISTRATION

Step-by-Step Guide to Copyright Your Film Without a Lawyer

In this Chapter you will find a step-by-step guide to registering a film for copyright and step-by-step instructions to open a free eCO Electronic Copyright account with the USCO.

The Forms Bank in the back of the book offers sample filled-in paper copyright registration forms for a film and a storyboard. The Forms Bank also provides step-by-step instructions to complete Form PA for a motion picture, music video, "making of," "behind the scenes" or other audiovisual work and Form VA for a storyboard, photograph, character design, film poster, and other works of visual art.

The USCO offers a convenient electronic copyright registration method using the eCO portal for Electronic Copyright on the USCO website, www.copyright.gov. Registration of a work of authorship may also be filed by mail or hand delivery of paper forms to the U.S. Copyright Office.

Each work that is filed for copyright with the USCO is reviewed prior to accepting and registering it. Once the copyrighted work is registered, the application and all of the information contained therein becomes public record on the USCO website.

Below you will find instructions and step-by-step guides to:
- Register a free electronic account on eCO with the USCO, and
- Complete an electronic copyright registration for your film as a motion picture or other audiovisual work.

A filmmaker may file an application for copyright registration any time within the copyright duration, as discussed in Chapter 7. Prior to 1978, the law required any copyrighted unpublished work to be registered again upon publication. The current law does not require registration again upon or after publication, although the copyright owner may choose to do so.

Registration that is made within three months after publication of the work or prior to any infringement of the work, as discussed in Chapter 6, makes available statutory damages and attorney's fees to the copyright owner in court litigation. Without registration during that period or prior to infringement, only actual damages of the owner and profits of the infringer could be awarded in a court action, which may be considerably less.

This Chapter provides information about the USCO as well as a step-by-step guide to opening a free account for unlimited use. The USCO website, www.copyright.gov, is one of the greatest resources for a filmmaker, and is completely free to use for research, notices, press releases, legal updates and the like. Fees are charged for registration of copyrights, USCO-provided research and more, but minimal for the value and cheap protection, they provide great value.

A filmmaker's first actions after creating his work and fixing it in a tangible medium of expression should be placing a notice of copyright on his film and then copyrighting the work with the USCO. A filmmaker may also wish to copyright the film design elements created for his film if he owns them by virtue of his design or the design of an artist under a work-for-hire agreement.

The USCO was created in 1897 by Congress and was instituted as a separate department of the Library of Congress. Each year hundreds of thousands of applications for copyright are reviewed by the USCO. The USCO answers numerous inquiries by telephone, email and in person at its office in Washington, D.C. Additionally the USCO performs many legal and policy-related functions as stipulated by Congress.

The USCO provides online services to register for a free eCO account, which allows for electronic filing of copyrights. Anyone may access USCO online records without registering for an account, and such online research is free to the public. How to research records or obtain copyright research from the USCO is found in Chapter 14. See below for a step-by-step guide to registering for an eCO account with the USCO.

ELECTRONIC eCO ACCOUNT

The U.S. Copyright Office offers the opportunity to create a free electronic account on eCO, the "Electronic Copyright Office" copyright registration portal. The USCO does not charge a fee to open such account, which enables an applicant to register copyrights online and make electronic deposits, that is, submissions of the work being registered with the USCO. Other benefits of registering a work for copyright using an eCO account include lower filing fees and quicker processing time than for paper forms.

The USCO recommends before you register with eCO that you verify your internet browser or computer settings, disable the pop-up blocker and any toolbars from third parties, and set your privacy and security settings to medium. Currently the eCO system has been verified for use with Firefox browsers on the Microsoft Windows 7 Operating System. Registrants accessing eCO using other browsers might experience less than the most favorable response. Follow these easy steps to register and open an eCO account on the USCO home page, www.copyright.gov:

- Click, "Register a Copyright" then, "Log into eCO,"
- Click, "if you are a new user, click here to register,"
- Create your account with a user name and password,
- Continue to the next page to start a registration, or log out to return later to start a registration, or
- Bypass the first two steps above by linking directly to the www.eco.copyright.gov and register as a new user.

For more, see www.copyright.gov/eco/eco-tutorial-standard.pdf.

ELECTRONIC COPYRIGHT REGISTRATION

Registration is the process of filing a claim for copyright with the USCO using either paper forms or electronic registration via eCO, the Electronic Copyright Office. The Copyright Office encourages electronic

registration and provides the author of the work numerous benefits over paper registrations, including the following:
- Quicker processing times, currently 8 months compared to 13 months for paper filings
- Lower filing fees, currently $35 for a single author registering one work under his legal name, and otherwise other fees apply,
- Electronic uploads of deposits of many, though not all, works,
- Secure payment by credit and debit cards, electronic checks and USCO accounts, compared to only money orders and checks for paper registrations, and
- Online tracking status.

Electronic registration may be made for basic claims for each of the individual types of works of authorship:
- Work of the performing arts, motion pictures and other audiovisual works like music videos, "making of" and "behind the scenes" films and videos,
- Single issue serial,
- Sound recording,
- Literary work, and
- Work of the visual arts like storyboards, original art used in a film, on-set photographs and film posters.

Any filing for copyright with the USCO is a public record. Copyright applications that are accepted are accessible on the USCO website.

Registration is not necessary for copyright protection since copyright exists in an original work of authorship when it is fixed in a tangible medium of expression. However, an author may file to register his work for copyright anytime within the life of the copyright. Basic claims that can be registered for USCO copyright include:
- A single original work of authorship,
- Multiple unpublished works as an unpublished "collection," so long as all the works are organized in an orderly collection with one single title and one single author, or if multiple authors, then at least one single author is a copyrightable author contributing copyrightable work to each of the works, and

- Multiple unpublished works if they are all owned by the same copyright claimant and published together in the same publication on the same date, and
- Serial newspapers and magazines, subject to certain conditions.

The two types of registration are:
- Electronic registration through eCO, and
- Paper registration via mail or personal delivery to the USCO.

Below and in Table 13-A are instructions for each step necessary to register using the electronic eCO portal a motion picture owned by the filmmaker, which is not a work-for-hire for copyright.

1. Step-by-Step Electronic Registration of a Film

On the USCO site home page, click, **Register a Copyright,** then **Log in to eCO**. In **Copyright Registration** click, **Register a New Claim,** then follow the instructions on Table 13-A which follows.

2. Finish an Incomplete eCO Registration

If you did not complete a registration but you saved your form before logging out, log back in to eCO to finish the form and:

- In **Check Registration Case Status**, click **Working Cases,**

- Click on the blue **Case Number** and **Complete the form,**

- "Click "**Submit**"(no changes can be made after this),

- Click **Add to Cart**, then make **payment,** and

- Make the deposit or print a shipping label for mailing.

Table 13-A
STEP-BY-STEP eCO COPYRIGHT REGISTRATION
Motion Picture (Contribution is Not a Work-Made-for-Hire)

Page/Menu/Topic	Fill in Blank/Box	Question
Registration Process Overview	YES YES YES	Single work All work by one Material by one author
Type of Work	Motion picture	Type of work
Titles (ADD for each)	Your Film Title(s)	Title
Publication/Completion	If NO, year created. If YES, date, country	Published? Year created Date, country
Authors (ADD for each)	Your Name U.S.A. (or other) Click YES or NO Click YES or NO Your Date of Birth	Name Citizenship/ Domicile Anonymous work? Pseudonymous work? Date of Birth
Work Created by Author	Click if applicable OR Click as applies	Entire Motion Picture or function
Claimants (ADD for each)	Name/ Organization Address	Person/entity claiming ownership
Limitations of Claim (use of Preexisting Material) or CONTINUE	Fill in if applicable Fill in if applicable Fill in if applicable	Material Excluded Copyright Registration #
Rights & Permissions	Fill in if applicable	Contact for film rights
Correspondent MANDATORY INFO	Name / Company Address & Email	Person the USCO can contact
Mail Certificate MANDATORY INFO	Name & Address (physical address)	To mail Certificate of Registration
Special Handling	Fill in if applicable Provide reason(s)	Special Handling Compelling Reason
Certification (Add NOTE if applicable)	Type your name, click Certification	Certify under penalty of perjury
Review submission	FINAL EDITS	No changes after this
Choose next steps (see Deposit Upload in book)	Back, Template, Save, Add to Cart	To edit, save, use for other films, pay

3. Deposit Upload - Electronic Deposits via eCO

Part of the registration process is the requirement to "deposit," or submit, a specified number of copies of the work. The following classes of works may be registered with electronic deposits:
- Unpublished works,
- Works published only electronically,
- Published works requiring ID material deposits see USCO Circular 01 in the Free & Almost Free Materials section in the back of the book for more information on ID material), or
- Published works for which there are special agreements requiring the hard copy deposits to be sent separately to the Library of Congress.

All other classes of works may be registered and the fee paid via eCO but require hard copy deposits of works being registered. Upload the copy of your work electronically as follows:
- Click the green button marked, **Select files to upload**,
- Browse, select your file, submit and click, **Start upload**, and
- After uploading click, **Complete your submission**.

Make only one upload of each electronic deposit.

4. Check the Status of an eCO Registration

After logging in to your eCO account:
- Go to **Check Copyright Registration Status**,
- Click **All Cases** for the status of each case,
- Closed cases are those which have been processed, and
- Working cases are those requiring completion.

5. Special Deposit Requirements for a Motion Picture

Motion picture deposits must be in an acceptable format for the USCO to view. Currently the USCO cannot view 1-inch open reel videotapes, D-2 and other digital videocassettes, and 8mm

videocassettes. Deposits in these formats as well as other motion picture deposits require a written description consisting of:
- The title and episode title, if any,
- The nature and general content of the program,
- The date of first fixation and if it was simultaneous with the first transmission,
- The date of first transmission, if any,
- The running time, and
- The credits appearing on the work, if any.

Other special deposit requirements for motion pictures are:

- **A Published Motion Picture Deposit Must Include:**
    - A separate description of the nature and general content of the work (shooting script, synopsis or press book), and
    - One complete copy of the work, undamaged and free of splices and defects that would interfere with viewing it.

- **An Unpublished Motion Picture Deposit Must Include:**
    - A separate written description of the work, such as a shooting script, synopsis or press book. and
    - A copy of the work with all visual and audio elements covered by the registration, or identifying material in lieu of an actual copy including: (i) an audio cassette or other phonorecord reproducing the entire motion picture soundtrack or other sound portion of the film and description of the film; or (ii) a set containing one frame enlargement or similar visual reproduction from each 10-minute segment of the film and a description of the film.

6. Uploading Multiple or Large Files

When uploading more than one file or large files, follow the same instructions as when uploading one file. Click **Select files to upload** up to a maximum upload size of 500 MB. If one or more of your files is larger than 500MB, compress them by zipping into one file or divide larger files into smaller ones each less than the 500 MB maximum. The USCO receives zipped file uploads more quickly than individually uploaded files. If neither solution works for you, mail or hand deliver the files in a hard copy format, packing the files carefully in a box so they are not damaged.

7. Acceptable Electronic File Types for Deposit

Not every category of work or type of file is allowed for electronic upload through the USCO eCO portal. Some works must be submitted in hard copy. The test for acceptable electronic submission is the "best version" of the work in the format in which the work is fixed as required by the USCO.

The USCO list of acceptable electronic files is below. The link is http://www.copyright.gov/eco/help-file-types.html. Files include:
- .avi (audio video interleave),
- .mov (QuickTime),
- .mpb, .mpeg (Moving Picture Experts Group),
- .rm, .rv (Real Media File),
- .swf (Adobe Flash, formerly Shockwave Flash), and
- .wmv (windows media video).

If the file you wish to upload is not an acceptable file type, convert it to one of the above. Any other file type will delay review and processing of your application, and could require the submission of another deposit in an acceptable format. Delays in processing also delay the effective date of copyright registration.

PAPER FORM COPYRIGHT REGISTRATION

If you choose not to register a copyright electronically using eCO, you may also register by mail or hand delivery using paper forms. Certain applications must be on paper and mailed or hand delivered to the USCO with the fee and deposit, such as Form CA for corrections and amplifications to a prior registration and Form RE for renewals.

The USCO provides copyright application forms online at its website, www.copyright.gov. On the USCO website click, "Forms" then click and open the Form you want. Each is a fillable form, but cannot be saved, so print out the Form after completion. Primary paper forms are:

1. Form PA (Performing Arts/Motion Pictures)

Form PA is used for works of the performing arts, motion pictures, audiovisual works and screenplays. This form refers to dramatic works intended to be performed before an audience. Examples of works copyrighted on Form PA include motion pictures, music videos, training films, workout films, corporate videos, commercials, "making of" and "behind the scenes" videos and screenplays.

Sounds and music accompanying motion pictures are included as a part of the copyright registration in Form PA, not Form SR.

See the Forms Bank for a Sample filled-in Form PA and instructions for any Form PA.

2. Form VA (Visual Arts)

Works of visual art are registered using Form VA. Filmmakers can copyright film-related works of visual art and pictorial, graphic and sculptural works, such as storyboards, fictional characters if designed, art painted for a film, film posters and elements such as photographs and designs, one-of-a-kind masks, photographs, unique tattooes, and other assets that a filmmaker can own and copyright.

The Forms Bank offers a filled-in Form VA and instructions to complete Form VA for acceptable works.

3. Form SE (Serial Publications)

Use Form SE to register a single serial publication, one that is numbered and dated in sequential order and is intended to be published indefinitely. Examples include comic books, newspapers, and magazines. A limited edition publication such as a six-book series is not copyrighted under Form SE, but rather Form TX.

4. Form SR (Sound Recordings)

Form SR is utilized for sound recordings but not motion picture soundtracks. Sound recordings include audio recordings of music only or of music and words. A musical score or a motion picture soundtrack created for a film is not copyrighted under Form SR. These works accompany motion pictures and are registered as part of the film on Form PA.

5. Form TX (Text, Literary Works, Software)

Form TX is used to register literary works of fiction and non-fiction, fictional characters if text-based and other works.

6. Form CO (universal Copyright application)

Form CO is a universal Form to register motion pictures and other audiovisual works or performing arts, visual works of art, single serial issues, sound recordings or literary works instead of the applicable paper Forms PA, VA, SE, SR, or TX. Form CO is processed quicker due to the imbedded bar code but the fee is the same.

7. Form CON (Continuation)

Form CON is for information that will not fit on any of the paper Forms, such as names and addresses of additional authors. Add the original Form letters in the upper right hand corner blank for this Form, such as PA-CON.

8. Form RE (Renewal)

Form RE is used to file renewals of copyrights. This Form is used for older copyrights that were registered under prior U.S. copyright law requiring renewal to preclude copyright expiration that would then place the work in the public domain.

9. Form CA (Correction and Amplification)

The USCO also allows a copyright registrant who wishes to correct or amplify a prior registration to file Form CA, a supplemental registration form. The information provided in Form CA adds to an earlier application, but does not supersede it. All information sent to the USCO is public record and later forms do not cause the deletion of earlier applications. Form CA is a supplemental form only and cannot be used as a substitute for an original or renewal registration.

LABELS, DEPOSITS AND SHIPPING

When you have complete the appropriate paper Form, obtain the shipping label and prepare the deposit, as follows:
- Click the button at the bottom of the page marked, "Create shipping slip,"
- When the slip is visible, click the blue shipping slip link to review and print out the slip,
- Attach it to the work you submit using paper applications or for hard copy deposits, and
- For multiple deposits, attach a *separate shipping slip* to each work or set of works you submit.

Follow the instructions on the Form to determine how many copies to send and in which format. To facilitate processing, the USCO requires that all required items for registration of a work be included in the same package, including:
- The completed application on the proper Form,
- The fee (nonrefundable), and
- The required number of copies as the deposit (nonreturnable).

Protect the work being sent as the deposit by mail or hand delivery. Due to enhanced security measures on Capitol Hill in Washington, D.C. envelopes may be damaged in handling. It is always prudent to mail or ship your work in proper packaging. The USCO recommends packing any of the following work in boxes, limiting each package to 20 pounds:

- Electronic media, including, but not limited to, CDs, DVDs, videocassettes, audiocassettes and the like,
- Microform (microfilm, microfiche),
- Photographs, and
- Print items of rubber and vegetable-based, such as color photocopies, glossy advertisements or prints, or posters.

Filing a copyright registration with the USCO using paper forms instead of electronic filing via eCO increased the processing time and the fees. The USCO will contact you by mail or phone with any questions regarding your application. Paper forms must be typed or completed in legible print rather than cursive with a black ink pen. Blank applications are available at www.copyright.gov or may be photocopied on a good grade of white 8.5" x 11" paper.

Applications that do not meet these criteria may be returned or cause delay in registration of the work. If you prefer to receive blank forms in the mail for completion by hand, the USCO provides a Forms & Publications Hotline at (202) 707-9100. The USCO limits each request to two copies of each Form by mail. Send paper applications and hard copy deposits to the Library of Congress, U.S. Copyright Office, 101 Independence Avenue SE, Washington, DC 20559. You will not receive an email confirmation or receipt notice of paper filings but can send a package by registered or certified mail and request a return receipt.

FEES FOR ELECTRONIC & PAPER REGISTRATION

The USCO charges nominal fees to file for copyright registration of a work. Fees vary depending on the type of work submitted, the author's status and other factors. The USCO also charges various fees for different services handled by the office.

Filing fees via an eCO account are lower in cost than paper registration, which also takes longer to process. Fees are non-refundable and are subject to change. Current USCO filing fees are:
- Basic Electronic Registrations:
    - Single Application (single author, same claimant, one work, not a work-for-hire): $35

- - Multiple Authors or works: $55
- Basic Paper Registrations:
  - Application using paper Form PA, Form VA, Form SE, Form SR and Form TX: $85
- Renewal Registrations:
  - For works published or registered before January 1, 1978 on Form RE: $100
  - Addendum to Form RE, in addition to fee for claim: $100
- Preregistration of certain unpublished works: $140
- Supplementary registrations:
  - Form CA: $130

Electronic filers may use credit cards, debit cards or ACH check payments to pay the fee on the eCO portal. Paper registration fees may only be made by a personal or company check, bank cashier's check or official check or bank money order, not international or postal money orders.

If a check for the filing fee is returned to the Copyright Office as uncollectible, the USCO will cancel the registration and advise the filer who must begin the registration process again and pay another fee.

You may register and pay the fees electronically even if a physical deposit is required. After filing the registration and making the payment, print a shipping slip and mail or hand deliver the physical copy of the work together with the slip.

COMMUNICATIONS WITH THE USCO

If you use the eCO portal, after you have filed your application, paid for and uploaded (or mailed or delivered) the deposit of your work for your claim for copyright, you will receive an email acknowledging receipt of your filing. Paper registrations do not receive any acknowledgements.

Several months after a filing is sent electronically or by paper registration, the USCO reviews the application and notifies if additional information or a file in acceptable format is needed. The USCO agent will contact you by phone, email or by letter.

Once the copyright is registered, the USCO sends the Certificate of Registration by mail. Letters rejecting the application are also sent by mail with reasons for not accepting the work for copyright.

Any USCO request for information sets a deadline for your response. If for a reasonable reason you cannot respond by the deadline, such as the inability to obtain the required information, illness or otherwise it is important to respond, explain the situation and request an extension.

Extensions are not automatic but may be granted for good reason. If you fail to respond by the deadline, or extension, your application may be considered abandoned and void. In this case, you must start the entire process again with a new application, fee and deposit.

To email the USCO, click, "Contact Us" at the bottom of the homepage, or call the Public Information Office at (202) 707-3000 or 1-877-476-0778 (toll free). It is important to avoid issues of non-receipt of USCO correspondence by maintaining current contact information on registrations. Use Form CA for address changes.

CERTIFICATE OF REGISTRATION

An important reason to register a work for copyright is the official Certificate of Registration issued by the USCO to the copyright owner as evidence of the copyrighted work. When the USCO has reviewed, and approved a copyright claim for registration, it issues such a Certificate.

This Certificate of Registration is official proof of ownership of his ownership of the exclusive rights in the work, which provides evidence if the owner brings a legal action for infringement. Such a Certificate also provides proof of copyright ownership to anyone who wishes to obtain a license to use an exclusive right or to acquire one or more exclusive rights through an assignment. The USCO mails the Certificate to the copyright owner at the address on the filing application. In the event a copyright owner changes his address, it is very important to notify the USCO. If the registration was made electronically, respond by email referencing the case number in the USCO email acknowledging receipt of the filing.

Processing time varies for copyright filings; however, electronic filings are reviewed more quickly than paper forms. Recently, electronic registrations took eight months and paper forms took thirteen. The effective date of registration is the date on which the USCO receives all the required materials -- application, filing fee and deposit of the work.

REGISTRATION AFTER PUBLICATION

Without copyright registration, the copyright owner can only be eligible for an award of actual damages, not statutory damages. A copyright owner who does not register his work created in the U.S. at the time of publication may still register the work for copyright within three months after the publication date and before an infringement on the work.

Such registration is prima facie evidence in court. "Prima facie" means the information on its face is valid and all facts stated in the copyright application are presumed true, without additional proof. These facts in the registration encompass all that the filer included in the document, such as publication date, registration date, certificate number, and owner, title and description of the work.

RECORDATION OF TRANSFERS

The USCO receives and records transfers of ownership of copyrights for a fee, retaining a true copy of the original. This serves as an authentic copy of the original, which is evidence in a court of law, such as in a claim of infringement or of ownership.

PREREGISTRATION

Certain unpublished works in specific classes of works and are being readied for publication through commercial distribution, may preregister for a fee of $140 per work on the eCO portal.

RENEWALS

Under U.S. copyright law, certain older copyrights of works created prior to January 1, 1978 are eligible for renewal filed by the current owner, claimant or agent on Form RE.

BEST EDITION

The USCO requires a deposit of one or more of the "best edition" of published works after January 1, 1978. General rules for deposits follow:
- Unpublished works: One complete copy of the work,
- Published works on or after January 1, 1978: Two complete copies of the best edition of the work,
- Published works before January 1, 1978: Two complete copies as the work existed at the time of its first publication, and
- Published work first published outside the United States: One complete copy as the work existed at its first publication.

eCO APPLICATION HARD COPY DEPOSITS

If you file your application using eCO and are required to send a physical copy deposit rather than, or in addition to, a digital upload of your work, a shipping slip printed from the eCO portal must be included with your deposit. This shipping slip may not be used again It connects a specific deposit with an electronic or paper application. If you sent multiple packages, number each package and the total number, such as 1 of 5, 2 of 5 and so on and attach the applications to the deposits.

FEDERAL REGISTER

The U.S. Copyright Office announces proposed rules, rules, announcements and other notices in the Federal Register, an official government publication published every day by the National Archives and Records Administration, at www.copyright.gov.

14. RESEARCH

Search for Copyrights Online or In-Person

Copyright registration and renewal applications and other related information are public record, which means anyone may search, review and inspect them. For filmmakers, producers, directors, film students, educators and others interested in researching copyrights that have expired and are in the public domain, or in finding contact information for a copyright owner to acquire or license the work, the U.S. Copyright Office provides a wealth of information at www.copyright.gov.

For example, a filmmaker might wish to find the copyright owner of a book to adapt into a screenplay and a film. Visit the USCO website and follow the simple steps in this Chapter to obtain the owner or the owner's agent and his last-filed address. This type of online research on the USCO website, www.copyright.gov, is free, quick and efficient.

To find a work copyrighted in another country, online accessibility to that information is subject to that policies of the copyright registry in that nation. If a CMO exists in the country where the filmmaker seeks information about a work, the organization can assist with obtaining authorization for the rights if the owner is a member of that CMO.

For people seeking specific information or documents relating to copyright, the USCO provides a choice of three types of research. The USCO website, www.copyright.gov, offers online research of registration applications, renewal information and recorded documents. For online self-research, no eCO Electronic Copyright Office account is required, nor is a fee charged.

Alternatively, instead of doing your own online research, the Copyright Office will search their records for you, for a fee. For in-person research, visit the Library of Congress and research the USCO records there.

USCO WEBSITE SELF-RESEARCH

The steps for researching copyright records on the USCO website are similar to those for online research on any site. However, an understanding of the USCO terminology and search parameters is necessary in order to be able to search efficiently. The USCO divides records into two time periods: (i) post-1978 records from 1978 to the current date, and (ii) pre-1978 records between 1860 and 1977. Each is described in a step-by-step guide below.

For any search visit the USCO website, www.copyright.gov, click the home page image, "Search Records," then choose the period for your search. Instructions on both searches are given below.

1. Post-1978 Records

Copyright records for the period from January 1, 1978 to the present are in machine-readable form and catalogued as "Post-1978 Records." From the USCO Home page click, "Post-1978 Records." Decide whether to do a "Basic Search" or an "Other Search" which is more advanced. Then click the relevant tab. Both types of searches are explained below.

- **Basic Search:**
    - On the Public Catalog page, fill in "Basic Search" box with term(s) you seek,
    - Select the category to search, and scroll down for "Search Hints" providing guidelines for each of these categories (Title, Name, Keyword, Copyright Registration Number, Document Number, Command Keyword),
    - Choose the number of records to display on a page (10, 25, 50 or 100); the site defaults to 25 records per page,
    - Hit the "Begin Search" button for results,
    - Results show the number per page and total records,

- On the results page, you can organize and re-sort files by Title, Name Date in ascending or descending order,
- Click on the number or title of any record to see its contents displayed on a new page.

As an example, type "Romeo and Juliet" in the "Basic Search" box, select Title, leave the default 25 records to a page and click, "Start Search." The results page displays as:

PUBLIC CATALOG
Copyright Catalog (1978 to present)
Search Request: Left Anchored Title = Romeo and Juliet
Search Results: Displaying 1 through 25 of 960 entries.

Your search "Romeo and Juliet" yields 960 copyrights and shows 25 of the total number of entries on the first page. For an advanced search, use "Other Search Options" tab, as explained below.

- **Other Search Options (advanced search):**
    - On the Public Catalog page, fill in one or both "Other Search" boxes with term(s) you seek,
    - Select a category to define the terms (any of these, all of these, as a phrase) for each box,
    - Choose the category to search (Keyword Anywhere, Title, Name Claimant, Name, Name Personal, ISBN-ISSN-ISRC, Notes, Organization, Series) per box,
    - Choose the relationship of the term(s) in the first box to be the term(s) in the second box (And, Or, Not),
    - Choose the number of records to display on a page (10, 25, 50 or 100); the site defaults to 25 records per page,
    - Click the "Begin Search" button for results,
    - The results show the number on the page and the total records returned for that search,
    - On the results page, you may organize and re-sort the files by Title, Name Date (ascending order and, Date (descending order),

o Click on the number or title of any record to see its contents displayed on a new page.

In this search, type "Romeo and Juliet" in the top box, select "all of these" and "Title." Click "AND" between the boxes. Type "William Shakespeare" in the lower box, select "as a phrase" and "Keyword Anywhere," leave the default 25 records and click, "Start Search."

PUBLIC CATALOG
Copyright Catalog (1978 to present)
Search Request: Builder= (Romeo AND and AND Juliet)[in Title (TKEY)] AND ("William Shakespeare")[in Keyword Anywhere (GKEY)]
Search Results: Displaying 1 through 25 of 173 entries.

Your search for the title "Romeo and Juliet" AND "William Shakespeare" displays only 173 entries, fewer than the Basic Search of "Romeo and Juliet" of 960 results.

BUT if you vary your search to "Romeo Juliet" in the top box (deleting the "and" between "Romeo" and "Juliet"), select "all of these" and "Title", then click on "NOT" between the two boxes and type "William Shakespeare" in the bottom box, select "as a phrase" and "Keyword Anywhere", the search yields 1,651 entries, below:

PUBLIC CATALOG
Copyright Catalog (1978 to present)
Search Request: Builder= (Romeo AND Juliet)[in Title (TKEY)] NOT ("William Shakespeare")[in Keyword Anywhere (GKEY)]
Search Results: Displaying 1 through 25 of 1651 entries

To eliminate unnecessary research or end up with fewer or more copyright references than you seek, be specific with your word search and use the proper category to find exactly what you want.

If you cannot find your requested record and the "Search Tips" section does not provide an answer, change any of the search limitations and start over. If too many results display for your use, consider setting Search Limits, explained below.

- **Set Search Limits.** For either a Basic Search or Other Search Options, restrict the search limits by Date or by Item Type (Recorded Documents, Texts, Serials, Dramatic Work of Music or Choreography, Maps, Sound Recordings, Sound Recordings and Music, Sound Recordings and Text, Computer Files, Motion Pictures, Visual Materials, Kits, Preregistrations, Cancelled Registrations and more). Select your choices of limiting your searches by:
  - Choose one or more "Item Types,"
  - Choose multiple item types by holding down the <Ctrl> key during selection,
  - Item Type "Canceled Registrations" cannot be limited by Date; all other Item Types can be limited also by Date,
  - Click on Set Search Limits, and
  - Wait for the message "Search limits are in effect until you click on 'Clear Search Limits,'" then begin the search. The Limits will apply to any searches you perform until you click "Cancel Search Limits" or close the browser.

2. Pre-1978 Records

The records of the USCO in the category of "Pre-1978 Records" are online in 660 Catalogs of Copyright Entries (CCEs) in volumes dating from July 1891 through December 1977. The USCO continues to digitize the records in reverse chronological order from the current records in this category.

You are able to search these records by publication date, title, author and class of material, noting that early copyright records were not kept in the same form as they are today. Some records display only authors and titles, without an index or registration number. Some works by a single claimant in various classes are listed together, rather than individually.

These volumes may not reflect the entire copyright record or the current ownership of the copyrighted work you seek. The CCE volumes include the original copyright registration records, but generally not subsequent transfers of ownership. You may contact

the USCO for additional records or request a search for the complete copyright records on a particular work or works. Follow this guide to search pre-1978 records:
- Visit the USCO website, www.copyright.gov,
- On the Home page click, "Search Records,"
- On the Search Records page click, "Pre-1978 Records,"
- On the Copyright Records page, the default is to "Collection," where you can search by Topic to the right, or above the volumes by Relevance, Views, Title, Date Published or Creator,
- Click, "Date Published" for descending chronological order from most recent to oldest volumes, or "Creator" for the author of the work, or "Title" for the title of the work
- Topics may include a particular work more than once under different titles. "Motion pictures" or "Film" are found in Topics including, but not limited to:
  - "Copyright Records - Motion Pictures,"
  - "Motion Pictures,"
  - " Copyright Renewal Registrations - Literature, Art, Film,"
  - "Copyright Records -Dramatic Compositions Motion Pictures," and
  - "Copyright Records - Dramatic Compositions, Motion Pictures, including List of Renewals,"
- Scroll down and click on the CCE volume for the time period you wish to search, and
- Open the volume and check the index, usually in the back of the volume, to find the page where the work is listed.

USCO IN-PERSON RESEARCH

If you prefer to do hands-on, rather than online, research, you may conduct in-person research of Copyright Office records and catalogs. Visit the Library of Congress Public Records Reading Room, Room 1m-404 at the James Madison Memorial Library, 101 Independence Avenue SE, Washington, DC 20559.

USCO FEE-BASED RESEARCH

USCO staff members provide copyright records research for a fee. Services include locating registrations, transfers, renewals and other copyright documents and the status of works, whether still in a valid term of copyright or expired.

To begin the process, contact the USCO to estimate a fee for the work you would like to have done. Currently, an estimate costs $200, which applies to any search fee charged. The current hourly rate is $200 for each hour of research and preparation of the research report, with a two-hour minimum search costing $400.

The hourly fee of $200 is charged for locating or retrieving USCO nonelectronic records with a one-minimum. To retrieve electronic records, the USCO fee is $200 per hour with a half-hour minimum. Time thereafter is billed at that rate in 15-minute increments. The cost of an additional certificate of registration is $40. The charge for record certification is $200, which is added to any other fees.

The Copyright Office will not search records to learn if a work similar to other works has already been registered. All prices are current, but are subject to change.

To request copies of USCO records, contact the Copyright Office Records Research & Certification Section at (202) 707-6850, by email at copysearch@loc.gov.

INTERNATIONAL COPYRIGHT LAW RESEARCH

The U.S. Copyright Office website provides information about the international treaties it has signed, including details and the signatory countries, but not information on IP laws of all nations.

The World Intellectual Property Organization ("WIPO"), World Trade Organization ("WTO") and United Nations ("UN") jointly offer a free electronic database called "WIPO LEX" at www.wipo.int/wipolex/en.

The site gives IP information on treaties and national laws of WIPO members.

COLLECTIVE MANAGEMENT ORGANIZATIONS

Collective management organizations (CMOs") are organizations that represent members, typically authors, performers, musicians, and filmmakers who own their works of authorship. CMO's may collect and distribute royalties to owners, act as an agent representing authors and also represent filmmakers in certain types of film distribution.

CMOs for performers, such as musicians, are often referred to as "Performing Rights Organizations" ("PROs"). Not every CMO performs every type of task and the responsibilities depend on the field in which the CMO operates.

Three U.S. CMOs representing filmmakers in non-theatrical distribution are Criterion Collection USA, Inc., Motion Picture Licensing Corporation ("MPLC") and Swank Motion Pictures, Inc. Contact information is in the References section in the back of the book.

15. PUBLICITY & PRIVACY RIGHTS
The Effect on Film Content

While the First Amendment to the U.S. Constitution grants the right of free speech, it is tempered by an individual's right of privacy and right of publicity. Publicity and privacy rights protect distinctive interests separate from copyright, which protects the work of authorship but not the human subject of the work.

A "public figure," like a celebrity or athlete, or a "public official," such as an elected government officer, by his very position and lifestyle is of public interest with little privacy. Such a person still has the right to privacy. However, the commercial use of such public person's name, likeness or other identifiable attribute without his express permission violates his right of publicity. While the right of privacy expires at a public figure's death, in many states his right of publicity is transferred to his estate.

Other legal protections for public figures and public officials include defamation and unfair competition, both of which are outside the scope of this Chapter and the rights of privacy and publicity.

To eliminate the risk of potential litigation, it is always prudent to negotiate a life rights agreement or a release for the rights to personal information about the person, including his name, identity, likeness, voice, biography or resume and life story details.

The rights of publicity and privacy are important for filmmakers because they could limit or prohibit the use of otherwise free content in a new work of authorship. The right of privacy is discussed below.

RIGHT OF PRIVACY

The right of privacy is the right of an individual to protect his personal life and activities in which he can reasonably expect privacy and which is not of public interest. The right of privacy is not a specific right guaranteed by the Constitution but has developed through interpretation of several Amendments into a person's right to be left alone. Legislation limiting third-party access to an individual's personal information has developed as a statutory right to privacy.

Upon an individual's death, his right of privacy terminates. However, in some states, the decedent's estate may have light rights to protect the individual's right of publicity or commercial use of any personal attributes and image. In such cases, a public domain photograph of a famous celebrity would not be able to be used without the written authorization of the estate, and generally compensation. A discussion follows on the right of publicity.

Filmmakers have many choices when making a film about these famous people. They can tell the story of actual events and activities in an accurate and truthful manner, or they can fictionalize events and characters. To protect against violation of privacy claims, filmmakers can select locations, time periods, events and character descriptions for the film that do not closely resemble or identify an actual living person and his life.

Nonetheless, a filmmaker can be liable for right of privacy violations of a public figure or public official if the filmmaker does any of the following acts:
- Portrays the person in a false or offensive light,
- Appropriates, or takes, the person's name or likeness, which causes the famous person distress,
- Publicly exposes embarrassing facts about the person, or
- Intrudes into his personal space, such as aiming a telephoto lens into a celebrity's back yard.

It is important to remember that people who are not public officials or public figures are individuals with a legal expectation of privacy. Any script written about them without their permission that meets the criteria above could expose the filmmaker to a lawsuit for right of privacy and possibly other violations. The right of publicity is discussed next.

RIGHT OF PUBLICITY

Public figures and public officials who have a lower expectation and right of privacy still have the legal right to publicity.

The right of publicity in the United States is the right of an individual to prevent the unauthorized commercial use of his name, image, likeness, voice or other recognizable attributes of his identity.

This gives celebrities, athletes, politicians and other well-known figures control over how their name and likeness are used in a commercial setting. They can license or refuse the use of their personal identity attributes for commercial purposes in their sole discretion.

The right of publicity is generally protected by state legislation or state common law, but not every state recognizes this right. In some states, violating the right of privacy is a tort, a personal injury to the person of invasion of their privacy.

Such injury is caused by the unauthorized use of a person's name or likeness, unreasonable publicity or intrusion into the person's private life or portraying the person in a "false light" which negatively impacts their reputation or standing.

In other states, unfair competition protects the right of publicity, prohibiting a person from giving the public the impression that a product is endorsed by an individual by the use of that individual's name, likeness, voice or other personal identifying marker.

Or, a person may be able to trademark his identity, protecting it by federal law.

An individual may be willing to license his right of publicity to others to use in commercial promotion of products and as the subject of a film.

If the person of interest for the film is deceased, some states require approval of the deceased person's estate prior to use of their image. In these cases, a subject's personal identity or persona cannot be exploited without the estate's written permission.

PROTECT YOURSELF & PROTECT YOUR SCRIPT

Protecting yourself and your work as a filmmaker is important and it takes skill to balance the desire for story with the legal rights of potential story subjects.

The best way to avoid any liability concerning rights of publicity and privacy is to engage an experienced entertainment attorney and a clearance company to verify that your film does not violate these rights. The clearance company should specialize in privacy and publicity right clearances, which are different from copyright clearances. You may also wish to obtain Errors & Omissions insurance for both the production company making the film and yourself as named insured parties.

Obtain a signed written release from any people who are subjects of your motion picture. The release authorizes the use of their name, image, likeness, biography, voice, and any other of their personal attributes you may use in your film. It is important to have these releases signed before casting and other development and pre-production activities begin. This will cover all possibilities, whether or not these subjects remain in the final version of the film.

When researching material for a film about the life of a living person, obtain a signed life rights agreement from such person. If the person is deceased, the right of privacy no longer exists but in some states the right of publicity is a legal right, protecting the right of publicity of a deceased public figure or public official, such as celebrities, athletes and politicians. Use of their name and likeness may require a license agreement from the estate of the deceased person prior to using the work to avoid violating the right of publicity.

The rights of publicity and privacy are important for filmmakers to understand. These rights can limit or prohibit the use of otherwise free content about interesting characters, living or not, in a new work of authorship.

16. BUSINESS ENTITIES
The Right Legal Structure for Your Film and Business

Now that you as a filmmaker know about copyright, how to protect your films and film-related design assets, it is important to consider what type of legal structure to use for your business. This Chapter discusses different business entities that can be formed for use as a production company or other entertainment business purpose. Information is also provided on the use and importance of a single-purpose-entity ("SPE") for a film production.

Filmmakers who prefer to remain sole proprietors without any legal entity will also learn about filing a business name, sometimes referred to as a "DBA" or "doing business as" for which a fictitious business statement is filed where they operate. The information herein will help a filmmaker choose the right legal structure to meet his particular production and business needs or to remain a sole proprietor.

TYPES OF BUSINESS ENTITIES

When choosing a type of business entity in which to operate, the key factors to consider are the filmmaker's personal needs, financial situation, tolerance for risk and arrangement with business partners, if any. The business entities that are typically used for production companies and for individual film productions include:
- Corporation,
- Limited Liability Company,
- Partnership, including General, Limited and Limited Liability Partnerships,

- Sole Proprietor / Fictitious Business ("doing business as"), and
- Single Purpose Entity ("SPE") / Single Purpose Vehicle ("SPV").

The general practice for filmmakers in the entertainment industry who intend to produce multiple films is to create a company, whether it be corporation, limited liability company, a type of partnership, or otherwise, as the main legal entity for operations. That entity will also own the copyrights and exclusive rights of the titles in the library of films made by the company. However, each individual film is usually produced through a separate and distinct legal entity, often a limited liability company, referred to as an SPE or SPV.

A description of each type of legal structure is found below. Legal entities are filed with the business filings office of a state Secretary of State ("SOS") or of the state business or economic development office. You will find a listing of contact information for each U.S. state SOS or business office in the References section at the end of the book.

1. Corporation

A corporation is a legal business entity that is separate and distinct from its owners, who can be businesses or people. Requirements for formation vary with each state, but generally a corporation name is required to end in "Inc.," "Incorporated," "Co." or "Ltd." This distinguishes a corporation from other types of business entities. The owners of a corporation are shareholders and persons who make management decisions are the directors, elected by the shareholders to manage as much or as little business as they decide. Typically, the directors elect the officers who perform day-to-day operations and make decisions in the best interests of the company.

The positive attributes of a corporation include that it can do most anything an individual can do legally such as borrowing or lending money, entering into and performing on contracts, filing suit and being sued, owning and disposing of assets and other benefits. A major benefit of a corporation is that it shields its shareholders against liability for the corporate debts and other financial responsibilities. If the corporation cannot pay its debts, creditors can look only to corporate assets for repayment, not to the shareholders, except in the case of fraud or illegality.

One negative aspect of a corporation is double taxation. The corporation pays corporate income tax on dividends paid to owners, who also pay personal income tax on those same dividends. However, corporations are generally taxed on income at a fixed corporate rate, which may be greater or less than an individual's income tax rate depending on taxable income, deductions and other factors. Another drawback of a corporation is the cost of annual renewals and reporting, which can be expensive.

2. Limited Liability Company

A limited liability company is a type of business entity that is separate and distinct from its owners, called members, who can be individuals or other businesses. Members who manage such a legal entity are called managers or managing members. The name of a limited liability company should end with either "Limited Liability Company," "LLC" or "L.L.C." to designate this type of legal entity.

This type of business structure combines the benefits of corporations and partnerships. A limited liability company protects members from responsibility for company debt. It also creates a "pass-through" of income and expenses for each member according to the membership agreement instead of double taxation.

3. Partnership

A partnership is a business entity owned by two or more persons or other business entities, called "partners." Several types of partnerships exist, described below. The name of the partnership may end in "GP," "LP," or "LLP," with or without periods between the letters as the partners deem appropriate. In some jurisdictions, these ending initials are not required. Types of partnerships are:

- **General Partnership (GP).** In this entity, the owners are all general partners who share equally in the management, profits and liabilities of the partnership. In this partnership, none of the partners are protected from liability for the partnership's debts.

- **Limited Partnership (LP)**. This entity requires one or more general partners to be responsible for management and debts of one or more limited partners who make no management decisions. Limited Partners are not liable for debts of the entity, except as stated in the articles of partnership that generally limit their liability to their capital investment.

- **Limited Liability Partnership (LLP)**. The owners of this entity, or "partners," may be shielded from liability or not, depending on state regulations. In some states, this entity may only be formed by certain professionals like lawyers, accountants and architects, while in others anyone may form and own it.

4. Sole Proprietor / Fictitious Business ("DBA")

A sole proprietor is simply an individual who operates one or more businesses without forming a legal business entity. The owner may operate under his own name or may file a fictitious business statement, otherwise known as a "DBA" or "doing business as." This statement is a filing of a business name under which the sole proprietor will operate and with which the public can identify him.

A fictitious business statement is generally filed in a city or county, or a parish in Louisiana. Filing involves publishing a public notice about the formation of the business and its owner, often in the "Legal News" sections of local newspapers.

A benefit of operating as a sole proprietor is that there are no formal legal requirements. Even the fictitious business statement is optional. However, if a filmmaker does operate his business under a name other than his own, in many locations he is required to file a fictitious business statement. Filmmakers include their business income and expenses on Schedule C of their personal federal Form 1040 tax return.

The major drawback of a sole proprietorship, with or without a fictitious business name, is that the owner is responsible for all debts. There is no shield or protection against business liabilities. Creditors can sue the sole proprietor personally for non-payment of debts and can collect on a judgment by seizing personal property including his car, real estate, bank accounts and other assets.

5. Single Purpose Entity/Single Purpose Vehicle

For filmmakers, producers and others who produce and own their own films, a Single Purpose Entity ("SPE"), sometimes called a Single Purpose Vehicle ("SPV") is an important legal vehicle limiting production liability for filmmakers. The SPE pays debts and is the entity that is sued for claims relating to the film. Copyrights in the film, including under work-for-hire agreements, are assigned to the filmmaker's holding company that handles day-to-day operations. SPEs are created for each film that is produced and exist until the film is completed and transferred to the holding company. The SPE pays final bills, files a final tax return and is dissolved. A new SPE is created and the process is repeated for each new film.

HOW TO FORM A BUSINESS ENTITY

Most American state Secretary of State offices are generally responsible for accepting filings for new business entities in the state. These include corporations, limited liability companies, general or limited or limited liability partnerships and others to do business in the state.

However, after forming a new business, the owner must fulfill a number of conditions before starting to do business. An agent for service of process who lives in the state and has a physical address must be appointed to accept service in the event of litigation against the company. The owner must select management, such as directors for a corporation, managing partners for a partnership or managing members for a limited liability company. The initial meeting of the owner or owners of the company should be held and written minutes of the meeting kept for a record of all management decisions for the company.

A new business entity must also obtain a federal EIN (Employer identification Number) from the Internal Revenue Service and a state tax number for quarterly and annual tax returns from the state tax authority. States usually grant sales tax exemption certificates to businesses that buy materials for later resale. Filmmakers could be exempt from paying taxes on DVD materials for duplication, or on other goods for resale.

Numerous filings are also required, such as annual renewal filings, annual reports, franchise filings and other reports and fee payments necessary to maintain the entity's good standing. Depending on the entity's income and assets in the state, together with other criteria, these fees and costs can range from about $25 to thousands of dollars per year.

Local jurisdictions within a state may have additional requirements such as an operational license, or occupational licenses for the physical location of the business. In some states, such licenses are issued by a city. In others they may be under the authority of a county. Prior to transacting any business in any location, an owner should verify all tax and license requirements.

Filmmakers can choose from a variety of legal business structures under which to operate, produce, own and exploit films and their exclusive rights. Or they can operate as sole proprietors under their own names, or they can file a fictitious business statement and begin operating under an invented company name.

Your preferred business model should be based on your individual business goals as you build wealth in entertainment through Intellectual Property.

17. 2021 LEGISLATIVE UPDATE: Small Claims

NEW for 2021! This 2nd Edition provides information about the Copyright Alternative in Small-Claims Enforcement Act ("CASE"). This new legislation, signed into law by President Donald Trump in December 2020, provides an alternative forum to lengthy, expensive litigation in federal court for infringement cases.

The CASE Act established a Copyright Claims Board in the U.S. Copyright Office to provide copyright owners and alleged infringers with a procedure for resolving their claims. For small corporate or individual copyright owners, this new legislation provides an additional opportunity to resolve copyright claims of infringement.

This Claims Board functions similar to a small claims court and the staff assigned to the Board hear claims brought by copyright owners or alleged infringers within three (3) years of the date the claim accrued.

The Board is authorized to render legal determinations regarding the following claims, counterclaims and defenses, subject to certain legislative limitations and regulation requirements, including the following:

1. A claim for infringement of an exclusive right in a copyrighted work by the owner at the time of the infringement for which the claimant seeks damages, if any;

2. A claim for a declaration of noninfringement of an exclusive right in a copyrighted work; and,

3. A claim for misrepresentation in connection with a notification of claimed infringement or a counter notification seeking to replace removed or disabled material, with remedies limited to those in the Act.

The Act allows parties to "voluntarily seek to resolve certain copyright claims regarding any category of copyrighted work." After receiving notice, if either party chooses to opt out of the process, the Board is unable to proceed.

However, if the Claims Board does proceed, it is authorized to decide the case and award actual damages and profits, or statutory damages, subject to these restrictions:

- For works timely registered for copyright pursuant to certain legislation and eligible for statutory damages, such damages may not exceed $15,000 for each work infringed, up to a maximum of $30,000 in a single proceeding; or

- For works not timely registered for copyright pursuant to certain legislation and eligible for statutory damages, such damages may not exceed $7,500 for each work infringed with a maximum of $15,000 in any single proceeding.

While the Act does not generally grant authority for the Claims Board to award attorney fees and costs to the prevailing party, one exception is stipulated. These fees and costs may be charged against a failing party for "bad faith conduct." Otherwise, the parties are responsible for their own legal fees and other costs.

Copyright owners have the Copyright Claims Board as an additional method of resolving disputes that offers an alternative to litigation. The USCO website at www.copyright.gov provides additional information and details about the Board and procedures.

18. CONCLUSION

That's a Wrap!

In this *Copyright Handbook for Films* you have learned what copyright is and how it works, who can copyright and own a film, and the powerful asset of copyright created by history and law.

The book also covered the exclusive rights of copyright in a work and how they can be exploited, copyright duration, infringement and multiple methods of resolving infringement claims, both in court and using ADR in lieu of litigation. And the CASE Act offers yet another!

Fair use was also presented, including conditions for the legal use of copyrighted work without the author's permission. Numerous resources were provided of free content in the public domain, and free and almost free works in the public commons. The types of licenses used in the commons were also explained. The Visual Artists Right Act and moral rights of owners of VARA were presented as well as copyrightable design assets that filmmakers own and can copyright.

The Digital Millennium Copyright Act was explored, including digital infringement notice-and-takedown provisions, online service provider agents and what to do about an infringer's counter-notice.

International IP agreements and protections granted by many countries to U.S. copyrighted work were presented. Invaluable step-by-step guides showed you how to register for an electronic eCO account, register your works for copyright, and research online copyright information. You also learned about the rights of privacy and publicity. Finally, numerous legal structures were explained for you to find the right one for your film and your business.

Armed with this new intelligence, today is the day for you to begin your mission. It is time to protect your works and build wealth in the industry by copyrighting and exploiting the exclusive rights of your films and your film-related design assets. *Happy copyrighting!*

FORMS BANK

Instructions and samples follow of filled-in copyright paper Form PA for a motion picture and Form VA for a drawing of a storyboard. Download blank forms at www.copyright.gov, "Forms & Publications." Se Chapter 13 for required deposits for registrations. Use Form PA for:
- Motion pictures & other audiovisual works,
- Published or unpublished works of the performing arts,
- Dramatic works with music (screenplay, synopses, treatment),
- Musical works with accompanying words, and
- Pantomimes & choreographic works.

Use Form VA for these works:
- Published or unpublished works of the visual arts, and
- Pictorial, graphic or sculptural works, including photographs, prints & art reproductions, 2-D and 3-D fine, graphic and applied art, maps, globes, charts, technical drawings, diagrams, models.

- **Example 1: Register Film on Form PA**

    Filmmaker, Robin Montana (a pseudonym for Robin Marie Jones), a U.S. citizen, was born on January 1, 1990. She wrote and copyrighted her screenplay entitled "Never 2 Boring Days" and adapted the screenplay into a film with the same title. All film crew signed work-for-hire agreements and assigned all rights for their work to Robin. Robin does not have a separate production company and operates under her pseudonym for film registration purposes. The other pertinent information on the form is correct. Robin screened the film in Los Angeles for potential distributors on May 1, 2016, the publication date.

- **Example 2: Register Storyboard on Form VA**

    The filmmaker in Example 1, Robin Marie Jones, is an artist as well as a writer/director. She drew storyboard illustrations of characters and action sequences from the script for her film. She will copyright them with Form VA using her legal name. All the other information above and on the form is correct.

FORM PA REGISTRATION FORM FOR A MOTION PICTURE
Page 1 of 2
See Instructions to Complete Form PA on Page 186

Form PA
For a Work of Performing Arts
UNITED STATES COPYRIGHT OFFICE

REGISTRATION NUMBER

PA   PAU

EFFECTIVE DATE OF REGISTRATION

Month   Day   Year

Privacy Act Notice: Sections 408-410 of title 17 of the *United States Code* authorize the Copyright Office to collect the personally identifying information requested on this form in order to process the application for copyright registration. By providing this information you are agreeing to routine uses of the information that include publication to give legal notice of your copyright claim as required by 17 U.S.C. §705. It will appear in the Office's online catalog. If you do not provide the information requested, registration may be refused or delayed, and you may not be entitled to certain relief, remedies, and benefits under the copyright law.

DO NOT WRITE ABOVE THIS LINE. IF YOU NEED MORE SPACE, USE A SEPARATE CONTINUATION SHEET.

1
TITLE OF THIS WORK ▼
"NEVER 2 BORING DAYS"

PREVIOUS OR ALTERNATIVE TITLES ▼

NATURE OF THIS WORK ▼ See instructions
MOTION PICTURE

2
NAME OF AUTHOR ▼
ROBIN MONTANA, A PSEUDONYM

DATES OF BIRTH AND DEATH
Year Born ▼   Year Died ▼
1990

Was this contribution to the work a "work made for hire"?
☐ Yes
☑ No

AUTHOR'S NATIONALITY OR DOMICILE
Name of Country
OR { Citizen of U.S.A.
    Domiciled in _____ }

WAS THIS AUTHOR'S CONTRIBUTION TO THE WORK
Anonymous?   ☐ Yes ☑ No
Pseudonymous? ☑ Yes ☐ No
If the answer to either of these questions is "Yes," see detailed instructions.

NATURE OF AUTHORSHIP Briefly describe nature of material created by this author in which copyright is claimed. ▼
MOTION PICTURE DIRECTING AND EDITING

NOTE
Under the law, the "author" of a "work made for hire" is generally the employer, not the employee (see instructions). For any part of this work that was "made for hire" check "Yes" in the space provided, give the employer (or other person for whom the work was prepared) as "Author" of that part, and leave the space for dates of birth and death blank.

NAME OF AUTHOR ▼

DATES OF BIRTH AND DEATH
Year Born ▼   Year Died ▼

Was this contribution to the work a "work made for hire"?
☐ Yes
☐ No

AUTHOR'S NATIONALITY OR DOMICILE
Name of Country
OR { Citizen of _____
    Domiciled in _____ }

WAS THIS AUTHOR'S CONTRIBUTION TO THE WORK
Anonymous?   ☐ Yes ☐ No
Pseudonymous? ☐ Yes ☐ No
If the answer to either of these questions is "Yes," see detailed instructions.

NATURE OF AUTHORSHIP Briefly describe nature of material created by this author in which copyright is claimed. ▼

NAME OF AUTHOR ▼

DATES OF BIRTH AND DEATH
Year Born ▼   Year Died ▼

Was this contribution to the work a "work made for hire"?
☐ Yes
☐ No

AUTHOR'S NATIONALITY OR DOMICILE
Name of Country
OR { Citizen of _____
    Domiciled in _____ }

WAS THIS AUTHOR'S CONTRIBUTION TO THE WORK
Anonymous?   ☐ Yes ☐ No
Pseudonymous? ☐ Yes ☐ No
If the answer to either of these questions is "Yes," see detailed instructions.

NATURE OF AUTHORSHIP Briefly describe nature of material created by this author in which copyright is claimed. ▼

3
YEAR IN WHICH CREATION OF THIS WORK WAS COMPLETED
2016   Year
Complete this information must be given in all cases.

DATE AND NATION OF FIRST PUBLICATION OF THIS PARTICULAR WORK
Complete this information ONLY if this work has been published.
Month MAY   Day 01   Year 2016
U.S.A.   Nation

4
COPYRIGHT CLAIMANT(S) Name and address must be given even if the claimant is the same as the author given in space 2. ▼
ROBIN MONTANA
44 PERCH WAY
LOS ANGELES, CA 90028

See instructions before completing this space.

TRANSFER If the claimant(s) named here in space 4 is (are) different from the author(s) named in space 2, give a brief statement of how the claimant(s) obtained ownership of the copyright. ▼

DO NOT WRITE HERE OFFICE USE ONLY

APPLICATION RECEIVED

ONE DEPOSIT RECEIVED

TWO DEPOSITS RECEIVED

FUNDS RECEIVED

MORE ON BACK ▶
• Complete all applicable spaces (numbers 5-9) on the reverse side of this page.
• See detailed instructions.   • Sign the form at line 8.

DO NOT WRITE HERE
Page 1 of _____ pages

FORM PA REGISTRATION FORM FOR A MOTION PICTURE
Page. 2 of 2
See Instructions to Complete Form PA on Page 186

	EXAMINED BY	FORM PA
	CHECKED BY	
	☐ CORRESPONDENCE Yes	FOR COPYRIGHT OFFICE USE ONLY

DO NOT WRITE ABOVE THIS LINE. IF YOU NEED MORE SPACE, USE A SEPARATE CONTINUATION SHEET.

PREVIOUS REGISTRATION Has registration for this work, or for an earlier version of this work, already been made in the Copyright Office?
☑ Yes ☐ No If your answer is "Yes," why is another registration being sought? (Check appropriate box.) ▼ If your answer is No, do not check box A, B, or C.
a. ☐ This is the first published edition of a work previously registered in unpublished form.
b. ☐ This is the first application submitted by this author as copyright claimant.
c. ☐ This is a changed version of the work, as shown by space 6 on this application.
If your answer is "Yes," give **Previous Registration Number** ▼   **Year of Registration** ▼
PA-1-222-333   2015

5

DERIVATIVE WORK OR COMPILATION Complete both space 6a and 6b for a derivative work; complete only 6b for a compilation.
Preexisting Material Identify any preexisting work or works that this work is based on or incorporates. ▼
SCREENPLAY, "NEVER 2 BORING DAYS"

6

See instructions before completing this space.

Material Added to This Work Give a brief, general statement of the material that has been added to this work and in which copyright is claimed. ▼
ENTIRE FILM VERSION OF SCREENPLAY

DEPOSIT ACCOUNT If the registration fee is to be charged to a Deposit Account established in the Copyright Office, give name and number of Account.
Name ▼   Account Number ▼

7

CORRESPONDENCE Give name and address to which correspondence about this application should be sent. Name/Address/Apt/City/State/Zip ▼
ROBIN MONTANA, A PSEUDONYM
44 PERCH WAY
LOS ANGELES, CA 90028

Area code and daytime telephone number (310) NUMBER   Fax number (   )
Email youremailaddress@gmail.com

CERTIFICATION* I, the undersigned, hereby certify that I am the
Check only one ▶
☑ author
☐ other copyright claimant
☐ owner of exclusive right(s)
☐ authorized agent of _____
Name of author or other copyright claimant, or owner of exclusive right(s) ▲
of the work identified in this application and that the statements made by me in this application are correct to the best of my knowledge.

8

Typed or printed name and date ▼ If this application gives a date of publication in space 3, do not sign and submit it before that date.
ROBIN MONTANA, A PSEUDONYM   Date MAY 15, 2016

Handwritten signature (X) ▼
☞ x Robin Montana

Certificate will be mailed in window envelope to this address:	Name ▼ ROBIN MONTANA Number/Street/Apt ▼ 44 PERCH WAY City/State/Zip ▼ LOS ANGELES, CA 90028	YOU MUST: • Complete all necessary spaces • Sign your application in space 8 SEND ALL 3 ELEMENTS IN THE SAME PACKAGE: 1. Application form 2. Nonrefundable filing fee in check or money order payable to Register of Copyrights 3. Deposit material MAIL TO: Library of Congress Copyright Office-PAD 101 Independence Avenue SE Washington, DC 20559-6230

9

*17 U.S.C. §506(e): Any person who knowingly makes a false representation of a material fact in the application for copyright registration provided for by section 409, or in any written statement filed in connection with the application, shall be fined not more than $2,500.

Form PA–Full Reviewed 09/2015 Printed on recycled paper   U.S. Government Publishing Office: 2015-xxx-xxx/xx,xxx

INSTRUCTIONS to COMPLETE FORM PA
See Filled-In Form PA on Pages 184-185

	Table FB-A	
	INSTRUCTIONS - FORM PA	
Space #	Subject	Information To Provide on Form
1	Title	Title of the work Any previous/alternative titles Nature of work (i.e., Motion Picture, Screenplay, Music Video, Audiovisual Work
2	Author(s)	Name of author Date of birth (year only) Work-made-for-hire? Employer is author Author's nationality or domicile Anonymous? Yes or No Pseudonymous? Yes or No Type of contribution (Motion picture editing & directing, Screenplay, Music video editing)
3	3a. Creation 3b. Publication	Year work was completed (creation) Month/day/year of first publication Country of first publication
4	Claimant(s)	Name & address of ownership claimant
5	Previous Registration	If previously registered, YES & a, b, and c If not registered, click NO & move to # 6.
6	6a & 6b Derivative Work 6b. Compilation	6a: Derivative work only: Describe preexisting work used or adapted for work (public domain or copyrighted) 6b: Derivative work or Compilation: list added new materials (new film version, revised screenplay, revisions throughout)
7	7a. Fee 7b. Correspondence	Fee: Deposit account if you have one Address for USCO correspondence
8	Certification	Type (author, owner, claimant, agent) Print or type name & date HANDWRITTEN SIGNATURE REQUIRED
9	Return Address	Name & Address to send Certificate

INSTRUCTIONS to COMPLETE FORM VA
See Filled-In Form VA on Pages 188-189

\	Table FB-B	
\	INSTRUCTIONS - FORM VA	
Space #	Subject	Information To Provide on Form
1	Title	Title to identify the work Any previous/alternative titles Nature of work (Watercolor drawing, Tattoo design, Graphic art, Photograph, etc.)
2	Author(s)	Name of author Date of birth (year only) Work-made-for-hire? Employer is author Author's nationality or domicile Anonymous? YES or NO Pseudonymous? YES or NO Nature of Authorship. Click applicable box
3	3a. Creation 3b. Publication	Year work was completed (creation) Month/day/year of first publication Country of first publication
4	Claimant(s)	Name & address of ownership claimant
5	Previous Registration	If previously registered, YES & a, b, and c If not registered, click NO & move to # 6.
6	6a & 6b Derivative Work 6b. Compilation	6a: Derivative work only: Describe preexisting work used or adapted for work (public domain or copyrighted)(Screenplay) 6b: Derivative work or Compilation: list added new materials (Drawing of character, Tattoo design, Storyboard, Photograph)
7	7a. Fee 7b. Correspondence	Fee: Deposit account if you have one Address for USCO correspondence
8	Certification	Type (author, owner, claimant, agent) Print or type name & date HANDWRITTEN SIGNATURE REQUIRED
9	Return Address	Name & Address to send Certificate

FORM VA REGISTRATION FORM FOR A STORYBOARD
Page 1 of 2
See Instructions to Complete Form VA on Page 187

Form VA
For a Work of the Visual Arts
UNITED STATES COPYRIGHT OFFICE

REGISTRATION NUMBER

VA   VAU

EFFECTIVE DATE OF REGISTRATION

Month   Day   Year

Privacy Act Notice: Sections 408-410 of title 17 of the United States Code authorize the Copyright Office to collect the personally identifying information requested on this form in order to process the application for copyright registration. By providing this information you are agreeing to routine uses of the information that include publication to give legal notice of your copyright claim as required by 17 U.S.C. §705. It will appear in the Office's online catalog. If you do not provide the information requested, registration may be refused or delayed, and you may not be entitled to certain relief, remedies, and benefits under the copyright law.

DO NOT WRITE ABOVE THIS LINE. IF YOU NEED MORE SPACE, USE A SEPARATE CONTINUATION SHEET.

1

TITLE OF THIS WORK ▼
STORYBOARD FOR "NEVER 2 BORING DAYS"

NATURE OF THIS WORK ▼ See instructions
STORYBOARD ILLUSTRATIONS

PREVIOUS OR ALTERNATIVE TITLES ▼

PUBLICATION AS A CONTRIBUTION If this work was published as a contribution to a periodical, serial, or collection, give information about the collective work in which the contribution appeared. Title of Collective Work ▼

If published in a periodical or serial give: Volume ▼   Number ▼   Issue Date ▼   On Pages ▼

2 a

NAME OF AUTHOR ▼
ROBIN MARIE JONES

DATES OF BIRTH AND DEATH
Year Born ▼ 1990   Year Died ▼

WAS THIS CONTRIBUTION TO THE WORK A "WORK MADE FOR HIRE"?
☐ Yes
☑ No

AUTHOR'S NATIONALITY OR DOMICILE
Name of Country
OR { Citizen of U.S.A.
     Domiciled in

WAS THIS AUTHOR'S CONTRIBUTION TO THE WORK
Anonymous? ☐ Yes ☑ No   If the answer to either of these questions is "Yes," see detailed instructions.
Pseudonymous? ☐ Yes ☑ No

NOTE
Under the law, the "author" of a "work made for hire" is generally the employer, not the employee (see instructions). For any part of this work that was "made for hire," check "Yes" in the space provided, give the employer (or other person for whom the work was prepared) as "Author" of that part, and leave the space for dates of birth and death blank.

NATURE OF AUTHORSHIP Check appropriate box(es). See instructions
☐ 3-Dimensional sculpture   ☐ Map   ☐ Technical drawing
☑ 2-Dimensional artwork   ☐ Photograph   ☐ Text
☐ Reproduction of work of art   ☐ Jewelry design   ☐ Architectural work

b

NAME OF AUTHOR ▼

DATES OF BIRTH AND DEATH
Year Born ▼   Year Died ▼

WAS THIS CONTRIBUTION TO THE WORK A "WORK MADE FOR HIRE"?
Name of Country
☐ Yes
☐ No

AUTHOR'S NATIONALITY OR DOMICILE
OR { Citizen of
     Domiciled in

WAS THIS AUTHOR'S CONTRIBUTION TO THE WORK
Anonymous? ☐ Yes ☐ No   If the answer to either of these questions is "Yes," see detailed instructions.
Pseudonymous? ☐ Yes ☐ No

NATURE OF AUTHORSHIP Check appropriate box(es). See instructions
☐ 3-Dimensional sculpture   ☐ Map   ☐ Technical drawing
☐ 2-Dimensional artwork   ☐ Photograph   ☐ Text
☐ Reproduction of work of art   ☐ Jewelry design   ☐ Architectural work

3 a YEAR IN WHICH CREATION OF THIS WORK WAS COMPLETED
Year ▶ 2015   This information must be given in all cases.

b DATE AND NATION OF FIRST PUBLICATION OF THIS PARTICULAR WORK
Complete this information ONLY if this work has been published.
Month ▶ MAY   Day ▶ 01   Year ▶ 2016
Nation ▶

4

COPYRIGHT CLAIMANT(S) Name and address must be given even if the claimant is the same as the author given in space 2. ▼
ROBIN MARIE JONES
44 PERCH WAY
LOS ANGELES, CA 90028

APPLICATION RECEIVED

ONE DEPOSIT RECEIVED

TWO DEPOSITS RECEIVED

FUNDS RECEIVED

See instructions before completing this space.

TRANSFER If the claimant(s) named here in space 4 is (are) different from the author(s) named in space 2, give a brief statement of how the claimant(s) obtained ownership of the copyright. ▼

MORE ON BACK ▶
• Complete all applicable spaces (numbers 5-9) on the reverse side of this page.
• See detailed instructions.   • Sign the form at line 8.

DO NOT WRITE HERE
Page 1 of ____ pages

FORM VA COPYRIGHT REGISTRATION FORM FOR A STORYBOARD
Page 2 of 2
See Instructions to Complete Form VA on Page 187

EXAMINED BY _____ FORM VA

CHECKED BY _____

CORRESPONDENCE
☐ Yes

FOR COPYRIGHT OFFICE USE ONLY

DO NOT WRITE ABOVE THIS LINE. IF YOU NEED MORE SPACE, USE A SEPARATE CONTINUATION SHEET.

PREVIOUS REGISTRATION Has registration for this work, or for an earlier version of this work, already been made in the Copyright Office?
☒ Yes   ☐ No   If your answer is "Yes," why is another registration being sought? (Check appropriate box.) ▼
a. ☐ This is the first published edition of a work previously registered in unpublished form.
b. ☐ This is the first application submitted by this author as copyright claimant.
c. ☒ This is a changed version of the work, as shown by space 6 on this application.
If your answer is "Yes," give: **Previous Registration Number** ▼   **Year of Registration** ▼
PA-1-222-333   2015

DERIVATIVE WORK OR COMPILATION Complete both space 6a and 6b for a derivative work; complete only 6b for a compilation.
a. **Preexisting Material** Identify any preexisting work or works that this work is based on or incorporates. ▼

SCREENPLAY, "NEVER 2 BORING DAYS"

b. **Material Added to This Work** Give a brief, general statement of the material that has been added to this work and in which copyright is claimed. ▼
ILLUSTRATIONS ON STORYBOARD OF CHARACTERS AND ACTION SEQUENCES FROM SCREENPLAY, "NEVER 2 BORING DAYS"

DEPOSIT ACCOUNT If the registration fee is to be charged to a Deposit Account established in the Copyright Office, give name and number of Account.
Name ▼   Account Number ▼

CORRESPONDENCE Give name and address to which correspondence about this application should be sent. Name/Address/Apt/City/State/Zip ▼
ROBIN MARIE JONES
44 PERCH WAY
LOS ANGELES, CA 90028

Area code and daytime telephone number   (310) phone number here   Fax number   (   )
Email youremailaddress@gmail.com

CERTIFICATION* I, the undersigned, hereby certify that I am the
check only one ▶
☒ author
☐ other copyright claimant
☐ owner of exclusive right(s)
☐ authorized agent of _____
Name of author or other copyright claimant, or owner of exclusive right(s) ▲
of the work identified in this application and that the statements made by me in this application are correct to the best of my knowledge.

Typed or printed name and date ▼ If this application gives a date of publication in space 3, do not sign and submit it before that date.
ROBIN MARIE JONES   Date MAY 15, 2016

Handwritten signature (X) ▼
X _Robin Marie Jones_

Certificate will be mailed in window envelope to this address:	Name ▼ ROBIN MARIE JONES
	Number/Street/Apt ▼ 44 PERCH WAY
	City/State/Zip ▼ LOS ANGELES, CA 90069

YOU MUST:
• Complete all necessary spaces
• Sign your application in space 8
SEND ALL 3 ELEMENTS IN THE SAME PACKAGE:
1. Application form
2. Nonrefundable filing fee in check or money order payable to Register of Copyrights
3. Deposit material
MAIL TO:
Library of Congress
Copyright Office-VA
101 Independence Avenue SE
Washington, DC 20559

*17 U.S.C. §506(e): Any person who knowingly makes a false representation of a material fact in the application for copyright registration provided for by section 409, or in any written statement filed in connection with the application, shall be fined not more than $2,500.

Form VA - Full   Rev: 05/2012   Print: 05/2012—8,500   Printed on recycled paper   U.S. Government Printing Office: 2012-372-462/60,211

REFERENCES

For information only – no affiliation with or endorsement by author or publisher.

U.S. GOVERNMENT OFFICES
1. Internal Revenue Service (IRS) - Employer Identification Number (EIN) - www.irs.gov - Click on "Tools" then "Apply for an Employer ID Number"
2. Library of Congress - www.loc.gov
3. Library of Congress Motion Picture, Broadcasting, Sound Recorded Division - www.loc. http://www.loc.gov/rr/mopic/
4. Patents/USPTO - www.uspto.gov/patent
5. Strategy Targeting Organized Piracy - www.StopFakes.gov
6. Trademarks/USPTO - www.uspto.gov/trademark
7. U.S. Copyright Office (USCO), Copyright Claims Board - www.copyright.gov
8. USCO Copyrights Forms & Publication Hotline - (202) 707-9100
9. U.S. Customs & Border Protection - www.cbp.gov

IP SUPPORT ORGANIZATIONS
10. Copyright Alliance - www.cbp.gov
11. Copyright Society of the USA - www.csusa.org
12. WIPO LEX countries with IP laws - www.wipo.int/wipolex/en/
13. World Intellectual Property Organization/WIPO - www.wipo.int
14. World Trade Organization/WTO - www.wto.org

ALTERNATIVE DISPUTE RESOLUTION/ADR
15. American Arbitration Association™ - www.adr.org
16. IFTA Arbitration™ - www.ifta-online.org/ifta-arbitration
17. JAMS - www. jamsadr.com

CMOs - FILM
18. Criterion Collection, USA, Inc. - www.criterion.com
19. Motion Picture Licensing Corporation - www.mplc.org
20. Swank Motion Pictures, Inc. - www.swank.com

CMOs/PROs - MUSIC
21. American Society of Composers, Authors & Radio Artists - www.ascap.com
22. BMI - www.bmi.com
23. SESAC - www.sesac.com

ENTERTAINMENT ASSOCIATIONS & ORGANIZATIONS

24. Academy of Motion Picture Arts & Sciences - www.oscars.org
25. Academy of Television Arts & Sciences *(see Television Academy)*
26. Alliance of Special Effects and Pyrotechnic Operators - www.asepo.org
27. Alliance of Women Directors - www.allianceofwomendirectors.org
28. Alliance for Women Sound Composers - www.theawfc.com
29. American Society of Cinematographers - www.theasc.org
30. Association of Film Commissioners International - www.afci.org
31. Association of Independent Commercial Producers - www.aicp.com
32. Association of Independent Video & Filmmakers - www.aivf.org
33. Association of Talent Agents - www.agentassociation.com
34. Box Office Mojo - www.boxofficemojo.com
35. Casting Society of America - www.castingsociety.com
36. Film Fatales - www.filmfatales.org
37. Film Festivals Information - www.filmfestivals.com
38. Film Festival Free Submission Platform - www.filmfestivals.com/en/blog/festivalexpress
39. Film Independent - www.filmindependent.org
40. Geena Davis Institute on Gender & Media - www.seejane.org
41. Harry Fox Agency - www.harryfox.com
42. Independent Film & Television Alliance - www.IFTA-online.org
43. International Alliance for Women in Music - www.iawm.org
44. International Documentary Association - www.documentary.org
45. International Federation of Film Producers Associations - www.fiapf.org
46. Internet Movie Database - www.imdb.com
47. Internet Movie Database Pro Version - www.imdbpro.com
48. Motion Picture Association of America - www.mpaa.org
49. Music Video Production Association - www.mvpa.com
50. National Association of Broadcasters - www.nab.org
51. National Association of Theater Owners - www.natoonline.org
52. National Film Preservation Foundation - www.filmpreservation.org
53. National Music Publishers Association - nmpa.org
54. New York Women in Film & Television - www.nywift.org
55. Television Academy - www.emmys.org
56. Television Academy/Students - www.emmys.org/membership/student

57. The Latin Recording Academy - miembros.latingrammy.com/es/join/voting
58. The Recording Academy - www.grammypro.com
59. The Recording Academy/Students - www.grammy.org/recording-academy/grammy-u
60. Rumblefish - www.rumblefish.com
61. Set Decorator's Society of America - www.setdecorators.org
62. Social media platform for filmmakers & festivals - www.Fest21.com
63. Stuntmen Association - www.stuntmen.com
64. Stuntwomen's Association of Motion Pictures, Inc. - www.swamp.com
65. Sundance Institute - www.sundance.org
66. Television Academy - www.emmys.com
67. The Numbers - www.the-numbers.com - for film financial analysis
68. United Stuntwomen's Association - www.usastunts.com
69. V10 Stuntwomen's Association - www.v10stuntscom
70. Women in Film - www.womeninfilm.org
71. Women in Film & Video of Washington, D.C. - wifv.org

ENTERTAINMENT GUILDS & UNIONS

72. Alliance of Motion Picture and Television Producers - www.amptp.org
73. American Federation Musicians - www.afm.org
74. American Federation of Television & Radio Artists - www.aftra.com
75. Animation Guild - www.animationguild.org
76. Directors Guild of America: www.dga.org
77. Intl. Alliance of Theatrical Stage Employees - www.iatse-intl.org
78. International Brotherhood of Electrical Workers - www.ibew.org
79. International Brotherhood of Teamsters - www.teamster.org
80. International Cinematographers Guild (Local 600) - www.icg600.com
81. Location Managers Guild International - www.locationmanagers.org
82. Motion Picture Editors Guild - www.editorsguild.com
83. Motion Picture Sound Editors - www.mpse.org
84. Producers Guild of America - www.producersguild.org
85. SAG/AFTRA Screen Actors Guild - www.sagaftra.org
86. Screen Actors Guild National Headquarters - www.sag.org
87. Writers Guild of America - www.wga.org

FIAPF - INTL FEDERATION OF FILM PRODUCERS ASSOC.

88. ARGENTINA - Asociacion General De Productores Cinematograficos
89. ARGENTINA - Instituto Nacional De Cine Y Artes Audiovisuales
90. AUSTRALIA - Screen Producers Australia
91. AUSTRIA - Fachverband der Film and Musikindustrie
92. BELGIUM - Vlaamse Onafhankelijke Film & Televisie Producenten v.z.w.
93. CANADA - Canadian Media Production Association
94. CHINA - China Film Producers' Association
95. CROATIA - Croatian Producers Association (HRUP)
96. CZECH REPUBLIC - Audiovisual Producers' Association (APA)
97. DENMARK - Danish Producers Association
98. EGYPT - Egyptian Chamber of Cinema Industry
99. ESTONIA - Estonian National Producers Union (ERPÃœ)
100. FINLAND - Suomen Elokuvatuottajien Keskusliitto (SEK)
101. GERMANY - Verband Deutscher Filmproduzenten Ev
102. GERMANY - Allianz Deutscher Produzenten - Film & Fernsehen e.V.
103. ICELAND - Association of Icelandic Films Producers
104. HUNGARY - Magyar Audiovizualis Producerek Szovetsege - MAPSZ
105. INDIA - Film Federation of India
106. INDIA - National Film Development Corporation Ltd.
107. IRAN - Iranian Alliance of Motion Picture Guilds- Khaneh Cinemandia
108. JAPAN - Motion Picture Producers Association of Japan
109. LATVIA - Film Producers Association of Latvia
110. NETHERLANDS - Film Producers Netherlands (FPN)
111. NIGERIA - Association of Nollywood Core Producers (ANCOP)
112. NORWAY - Norske Film , TV og spillprodusenters forening
113. RUSSIA - Film Producers Guild of Russia
114. SLOVAKIA - Slovak Audiovisual Producers Association (SAPA)
115. SPAIN - Federacion de Asociaciones de Productores Audiovisuales de Espana
116. SWEDEN - Swedish Film & TV Producers Association
117. SWITZERLAND - Association Suisse des Producteurs de Films
118. TURKEY - Film Yapimcilari Meslek Birligi - Fiyab
119. TURKEY - Sinema Eseri Yapimcilari Meslek Birligi - Se-Yap
120. TURKEY - Tesiyap Televizyon ve Sinema Film Yapimcilari Meslek Birligi
121. UKRAINE - The Association of Ukrainian Producers

122. U.S.A. - Independent Film & Television Alliance (IFTA)
123. U.S.A. - Motion Pictures Association (MPA)

FREE & ALMOST FREE MATERIALS
COPYRIGHT OFFICE INFORMATION CIRCULARS: www.copyright.gov

124. 1 (English) - Copyright Basics
125. 1 (Spanish) - Fundamentos de los Derechos de Autor
126. 1a - USCO A Brief History Introduction
127. 1b -Limitation on the Information Furnished by the USCO
128. 1c - Make Sure Your Application Will Be Acceptable
129. 2 - Publications on Copyright
130. 3 - Copyright Notice
131. 4 - Copyright Fees
132. 5 - How to Open and Maintain a Copyright Office Deposit Account
133. 6 - Obtaining Access to and Copies of Copyright Records and Deposits
134. 7b - Best Edition of Published Copyrighted Works for Collections of LOC
135. 7c - The Effects of Not Sending a Timely Reply to USCO Correspondence
136. 7d- Mandatory Deposit of Copies or Phonorecords for the LOC
137. 8 - Supplementary Copyright Registration
138. 9 - Work Made For Hire Under the 1976 Copyright Act
139. 10 - Special Handling
140. 12 - Recordation of Transfers and Other Documents
141. 14 -Copyright Registration for Derivative Works
142. 15 - Renewal of Copyright
143. 15a - Duration of Copyright
144. 15t - Extension of Copyright Terms
145. 21 - Reproduction of Copyrighted Works by Educators and Librarians
146. 22 - How to Investigate the Copyright Status of a Work
147. 23 - The Copyright Card Catalog & Online Files of the Copyright Office
148. 31 - Ideas, Methods, or Systems
149. 32 - Blank Forms and Other Works Not Protected by Copyright
150. 33 - Computing and Measuring Devices
151. 34 - Copyright Protection Not Available for Names, Titles, Short Phrases
152. 38a - International Copyright Relations of the United States
153. 38b - Copyright Restoration Under the URAA
154. 40 -Copyright Registration for Pictorial, Graphic, and Sculptural Works

155. 40a - Deposit Requirements for Registrations of Claims to Copyright in Visual Arts Material
156. 41 - Copyright Claims in Architectural Works
157. 44 - Cartoons and Comic Strips
158. 45 - Copyright Registration for Motion Pictures Incl. Video Recordings
159. 50 - Copyright Registration for Musical Compositions
160. 55 - Copyright Registration for Multimedia Works
161. 56 - Copyright Registration for Sound Recordings
162. 56a - Copyright Registration of Musical Composition, Sound Recordings
163. 61 - Copyright Registration for Computer Programs
164. 62 - Copyright Registration for Single Serial Issues
165. 62b - Copyright Registration for Group of Serial Issues
166. 66 - Copyright Registration for Online Works
167. 73 - Compulsory License for Making and Distributing Phonorecords
168. 74a - Make Statutory License Royalty EFT Payments via Wire
169. 74b - Make Statutory License Royalty EFT Payments via ACH Credit
170. 75 - The Licensing Division of the Copyright Office
171. 92 - (*Note: Link to Copyright Law on USCO website, multiple circulars*) Copyright Laws of the U.S., December 2011 (some law not included)

CREATIVE COMMONS COPYRIGHT MUSIC LINKS FOR FILMS

172. ccMixter - www.ccmixter.org
173. Free Music Archive - www.freemusicarchive.org
174. Jamendo - www.jamendo.com
175. Magnatune - www.magnatune.com/genres
176. BeatPick - www.beatpick.com
177. CASH Music - www.cashmuslc.org
178. SectionZ - www.sectionz.com/cc.asp
179. Opsound - www.opsound.org/pool/artist
180. Podsafe Audio - www.podsafeaudio.com
181. AudioFarm - www.audiofarm.org
182. Internet Archive's Netlabels - www.archive.org/details/netlabels

eBOOKS & FILMS

183. AudioBooksForFree.com - British audio book publishers
184. ClassicalArchives.com - Composer performances
185. Internet Archive.org - Millions of free books, movies, software, music

186. LiteralSystems.org - Human audio eBook readings
187. Librivox.org - Human audio eBook readings
188. ManyBooks.net - Free eBooks, mobile accessible
189. MobileRead.com - free eBooks in Sony ereader and Mobipocket format
190. Mobipocket.com - free eBooks in .mobi format
191. Outernet.is - Free broadcasts, educational content from space
192. Prelinger Archives - archive.org/details/prelinger - films & videos
193. Project Gutenberg (original) - www.gutenberg.org - Free eBooks in US
194. Project Gutenberg of Australia - gutenberg.net.au
195. Project Gutenberg of Canada - gutenberg.ca
196. Project Gutenberg of Germany- gutenberg.spiegel.de
197. Projekt Runeberg - runeberg.org - Nordic literature
198. Pulpwood Magazines - www.pulpmags.org - 1896 - 1946 pulp magazines
199. ReadingRoo.ms - Textual items for unlimited redistribution
200. thefifthimperium.com - hosts PG Science Fiction CD download
201. Wattpad.com - Thousands of free titles, including self-published
202. m.wattpad.com - Wattpad mobile accessible site

PUBLICATIONS & PAPERS

203. *Beyond Cinema* - www.afci.org/beyond-cinema
204. *Cinema Editor Magazine* - americancinemaeditors.org/cinemaeditor
205. *CMO Handbook* - www.collectingsocietieshb.com
206. *Deadline* - www.deadline.com
207. *Hollywood Reporter* - www.hollywoodreporter.com
208. *Emmy(R) Magazine* - www.emmys.com/emmy-magazine
209. *Filmmaker Magazine* - www.filmmakermagazine.com
210. *Grammy Magazine* - www.grammy.com/photos/read-grammy-magazine
211. *Indiewire* – www.indiewire.com
212. *Journal of Copyright Society of the USA* - www.csusa.org/?page=Journal
213. *Movie Maker* - www.moviemaker.com
214. *P3 Update Magazine* - www. p3update.com
215. *Produced By Magazine* - www.producersguild.org/?page=produced_by
216. *Protecting Creativity* - www.mpaa.org/protecting-creativity/
217. *Rights, Camera, Action! IP Rights and the Film-Making Process* - www.wipo.int/edocs/pubdocs/en/copyright/869/wipo_pub_869.pdf
218. *Screen international* - www.screeninternationalmagazine.com

219. *The Field Guide to Sponsored Films,* by Rick Prelinger, www.filmpreservation.org/userfiles/image/ PDFs/ sponsored.pdf
220. *The Independent Magazine* – www.independent-magazine.org
221. *U.S. Notorious Market Report* - https://ustr.gov/sites/default/files/ USTR-2015-Out-of-Cycle-Review-Notorious-Markets-Final.pdf
222. *U.S. Special 301 Report* (Watch Lists of countries with copyright piracy) - https://ustr.gov/sites/default/files/USTR-2016-Special-301-Report.pdf.
223. *Variety* - www.variety.com
224. *Why Copyright Matters*- www.mpaa.org/why-copyright- matters/#3

SECRETARY OF STATE OFFICES or BUSINESS SITES

225. Alabama - www.sos.state.al.us
226. Alabama - sos.alabama.gov
227. Alaska - www.commerce.alaska.gov
228. Arizona - www.azcc.gov
229. Arkansas - www.sos.arkansas.gov
230. California - www.ss.ca.gov
231. Colorado - www.sos.state.co.us
232. Connecticut - www.ct.gov/sots
233. Delaware - www.corp.delaware.gov
234. District of Columbia - dcra.dc.gov
235. Florida - dos.myflorida.com
236. Georgia - sos.ga.gov
237. Hawaii - portal.ehawaii.gov
238. Idaho - www.sos.idaho.gov
239. Illinois - ilsos.com
240. Indiana - www.in.gov/sos
241. Iowa - sos.iowa.gov
242. Kansas - www.kssos.org
243. Kentucky - sos.ky.gov
244. Louisiana - www.sos.la.gov
245. Maine - www.state.me.us/sos
246. Maryland - www.sos.state.md.us
247. Massachusetts - www.sec.state.ma.us
248. Michigan - www.michigan.gov/lara (Licensing & Regulatory Affairs)
249. Minnesota - www.sos.state.mn.us
250. Mississippi - www.sos.ms.gov

251. Missouri - www.sos.mo.gov
252. Montana - www.sos.mt.gov
253. Nebraska - www.sos.ne.gov
254. Nevada - www.nvsos.gov
255. New Hampshire - sos.nh.gov
256. New Jersey - www.nj.gov/njbusiness
257. New Mexico - www.sos.state.nm.us
258. New York - www.dos.ny.gov
259. North Carolina - www.sosnc.gov
260. North Dakota - sos.nd.gov
261. Ohio - www.sos.state.oh.us
262. Oklahoma - sos.ok.gov
263. Oregon - sos.oregon.gov
264. Pennsylvania - www.dos.pa.gov
265. Rhode Island - sos.ri.gov
266. South Carolina - www.scsos.com
267. South Dakota - sdsos.gov
268. Tennessee - sos.tn.gov
269. Texas - www.sos.state.tx.us
270. Utah - www.utah.gov/government/secretary-of-state.html
271. Vermont - www.sec.state.vt.us
272. Virginia - www.virginia.gov/Business/Business-One-Stop
273. Washington - www.sos.wa.gov
274. West Virginia - www.sos.wv.gov
275. Wisconsin - www.wdfi.org
276. Wyoming - soswy.state.wy.us

STYLE GUIDES FOR ATTRIBUTION
277. APA STYLE - www.apastyle.org
278. CHICAGO STYLE - www.chicagomanualofstyle.org
279. MLA STYLE - www.mla.org

INDEX

A

Access, infringement, 79, 86, 87
Acquisition, option and, 64, 68-70
Actual damages, 79-87, 94, 148, 162
Adapt, exclusive right to, 46; see also Derivative works
Agent, copyright owner, 38, 39, 67
Agent, service provider, 128, 130, 131
Alternative Dispute Resolution (ADR), 18, 86, 88
Anonymous work, 43, 98
Arbitration, 78, 89-92, 106
Assignment, 37, 39, 41-42, 46, 58, 64, 67-69, 92, 113, 161
Attorney's fees, 32, 74-75, 79-80, 82-86, 133-134, 140, 148
Attribution, author's name, 33
Attribution, fair use, 17, 58, 73, 95, 105-110, 115, 128, 173, 182
Attribution, VARA right of, 121-124
Audiovisual work, 14-15, 18, 25-26, 30, 40, 49-52, 62-63, 94, 123, 129, 143, 147, 150, 155-157; see also Film; Motion picture
Author, 16, 21-22, 27-29, 31, 33-35, 37-46, 48-49, 51, 69, 71, 73, 84, 97-100, 110-112, 119-124, 138-140, 143, 150, 157, 159, 168-171, 182; see also Claimant; Owner
Authorized use, 91
Authorship, 14-16, 20-46, 49, 52-53, 58, 63-64, 70-73, 85, 95-98, 101, 115, 119, 121, 138, 140-144, 147, 150, 162, 171-173

B

Berne Convention, 53, 119, 139-141, 143-144
Best edition, 29-31, 163
Bundle of rights, 17, 57, 73; see also Exclusive rights

C

Cease and desist letter, 77, 85-86
Certificate of Registration, 78, 86, 160-161, 170
Circular, USCO, 18
Claim, 34, 39-45, 49, 72, 78-91, 95-96, 119, 121, 124, 128-134, 149-151, 159-162, 173-174
Claimant, 38-39, 88, 151, 159, 162, 166, 168
Collective bargaining agreement, 89, 129, 133-134
Collective Management Organization (CMO), 18, 71, 170
Collective work, 40, 44-46
Comment, as fair use, 29, 95, 106-107
Commentary, as fair use, 106-107
Commons, 19, 112, 115-118, 182
Communication with USCO, 15, 86, 128, 130-131, 139, 160
Compilation, 28-29, 40, 44-46, 76
Compulsory license, 65, 67
Contributory infringer, 74-77, 83
Copy or reproduce exclusive right to, 57, 71, 78
Copyright, 13-23, 25-55, 57-101, 103-109, 111-113, 115-125, 127-135, 137-145, 147-151, 153, 155-177, 179-182

Copyright Act, 17, 50-52, 97, 127, 129, 182
Copyright Clause, 22, 48-49
Copyright Management Information (CMI), 127-129
Copyright notice; see Notice of copyright; Notice to the public
Copyright notice, fraudulent, 94
Copyright notice, fraudulent removal of, 94
Copyright Office, 14, 17-18, 25-26, 35-36, 38, 43-44, 49, 71, 78, 128, 147, 149, 159-165, 169-170
Copyright owner; see Owner
Copyright Term Extension Act, 50-51, 97
Copyright, when secured, 25
Copyrightable works, 13, 24, 35
Corporation, 60, 71, 114, 116, 171, 176-178, 181
Costs, 26, 65, 69-70, 74-75, 79, 83-86, 88, 133-134, 170, 177, 180
Counter notice, DMCA, 133, 182
Court order, 85, 87, 132
Creative Commons, 19, 112, 115-116, 118
Creativity, requirement for, 22
Criminal infringement, DMCA, 15, 17, 32-34, 49, 52, 59, 71-88, 91-96, 105-109, 124, 127-131, 138, 140, 148, 161-162, 182
Criminal proceedings, 25, 47, 88, 93
Criticism, as fair use, 95, 107
Critique, as fair use, 106-107
Damages, 25, 32-34, 49, 71-89, 93-95, 133, 140, 148, 162, 174; see also Actual damages; Statutory damages

D

Defendant's profits; see Profits, damages for infringement
Defenses to infringement, 73
Deposit, digital upload, 137, 163
Deposit, Mandatory, 31
Deposit, physical copy, 163
Deposit, published work, 29
Deposit, special rules for motion picture, 29-30
Deposit, unpublished work, 30
Derivative works, 25, 28, 38, 46, 57-58, 63-64, 68, 95, 113; see also Adapt, exclusive right to
Design assets, film-related, 119, 176, 182
Designs, copyrightable, 120
Device, machine or process, 62-63
Digital Millennium Copyright Act (DMCA), 17, 51-52, 127-129, 182
Digital Rights Management (DRM), 83, 128-129
Display, exclusive right to, 57-58, 61-63
Distribute, exclusive right to, 60, 65
DMCA; see also Digital Millennium Copyright Act (DMCA)
Doing business as, 176-177, 180; see also Fictitious business statement
Duration for joint works, 124
Duration, 1909 Copyright Act, 97
Duration, 1988 CTEA, 97
Duration, Anonymous work, 98
Duration, Author, 140
Duration, Joint authors, 124
Duration, Renewal, 51

E

ECO account, 148-151, 159, 182
ECO tutorial, 149
Education, as fair use, 106, 108, 114-115, 118
EIN (Employer ID Number), 181
Electronic files for deposits, 76, 155
Electronic registration, 149-151, 159, 161
Employment agreement, 37, 40
Exclusive license, 65-68, 91-92, 96
Exclusive rights, 17, 37-41, 43, 47, 57-60, 63-71, 73-74, 77-78, 82, 87, 91-92, 96, 100-101, 108, 115,119-122, 124, 128-129, 161, 177, 181-182
Exemption to exclusive right to copy or reproduce, 71
Expression of idea, 21, 24
Extensions, copyright duration, 51, 97

F

Fair use, 17, 58, 73, 95, 105-110, 115, 128, 173, 182
False representation, 94
Family Entertainment & Copyright Act of 2005, 52
FEDFLIX, 19, 114
FEDLINK, 114-115
Fees, electronic copyright registration, 17, 147, 149
Fees, paper form copyright registration, 25, 155

Fictional characters, 23, 119-120, 156-157
Fictitious business statement, 179-180
File sharing, 74, 76, 79; see also Peer-to-peer sharing (P2P)
Film, 13-43, 45-95, 97, 99-182; see also Motion picture
Filmmaker, 13-19, 22-29, 35, 38, 41-42, 47, 49, 52-54, 57-75, 79, 89, 96, 105, 113-122, 127-129, 137-139, 148, 156, 164, 171-177, 180-181
Fine art, VARA, 21, 119-120, 123
First sale doctrine, 70, 77-78, 122, 128
Fixed, 20-25, 40-41, 46, 86, 150; see also Tangible medium of expression
Foreign authors, 44, 100, 143
Form CA, 155, 157, 160-161
Form CON, 27, 157
Form PA, 18, 26, 147, 155-156, 159
Form RE, 155, 157, 159, 163
Form SE, 27, 156, 159
Form SR, 26, 156, 159
Form TX, 26, 156-157, 159
Form VA, 18, 26, 119, 147, 156, 159, 180
Forms Bank, 17-18, 26, 147, 156
Forms, copyright, 155
Forms, filled-in paper forms, 147; see also Forms Bank
Four factors of fair use, 106
Freedom of Information Act, 54

G

General Agreement on Tariffs and Trade (GATT), 140
General partnership, 179

I

Idea, not copyrightable, 21
Immoral works; see Indecent or immoral work
Indecent or immoral work, 27
Independence of protection; 140, 143
Independent creation, 86, 96
Infringement, 15, 17, 32-34, 49, 52, 59, 71-88, 91, 93, 95-96, 105-106, 108-109, 124, 127-131, 138, 140, 148, 161-162, 182
Infringement action; see Litigation
Infringement defenses; see Defenses to infringement
Infringement remedies; see Remedies for infringement
Infringing acts, 75, 79-81, 83, 86, 91, 93, 95, 127
Injunction, 85-87, 132
Innocent infringer, 74-75
Integrity, VARA right of, 122
Intellectual property, 13, 20, 27, 29, 42, 49-53, 71, 87, 90, 92, 95, 119, 127, 137-143, 170; see also IP
International agreements, 52, 134, 138-139, 144, 182
International copyright, 17, 29, 135, 137-138, 170
Internet Archive, 114
IP, 13-15, 18, 49-54, 57, 138-139, 142, 144, 170; see also Intellectual property

J

Joint authors, VARA, 43, 98, 124
Joint work, 28, 43-44, 98, 124

L

Legal structures, 181
Legend, 32, 59; see also Notice of copyright
Liability limits for service providers, DMCA, 128
Liability, infringement, 128
Library of Congress, 29, 31, 113-114, 148, 153, 159, 165, 169
License, 37, 45-46, 57-60, 63-72, 86, 91-92, 96, 111-118, 161, 164, 174-175, 181-182
Limited liability company, 177-181
Limited liability partnership, 177, 179, 181
Limited partnership, 179
Literary work, 26, 150, 157
Litigation, 86
Losses, damages for infringement, 33

M

Making-of videos or films, 13-14, 20, 26, 147, 150, 156
Mandatory deposit, 29, 31
Mediation, 88, 90, 92
Merger doctrine, 21
Minors as authors, 44
Moral rights, copyright author, 21, 68, 119-120, 144, 182
Motion picture, 13-14, 18, 20, 24, 26, 29-30, 37, 40, 49-52, 62-63, 71-75, 93-94, 110-111, 123, 129, 133-134, 139, 147, 150-157, 168-169, 171; see also Film

Movie; see Film; Motion picture
Movie posters, 15
Music videos, 13-14, 20, 26, 49, 150, 156

N

National treatment, 140, 143
News reporting, as fair use, 95, 108
Non-exclusive license, 65-67, 91-92, 96
Noncopyrightable works, 24
Notice of copyright, 32-34, 75, 77, 94, 142, 148
Notice to the public, 16, 32-34, 77; see also Notice of copyright
Notice-and-takedown, DMCA, 129, 131

O

Option, 58, 61, 63-64, 68-70, 88, 93, 166, 168
Option and acquisition, 64, 68-70
Owner, 13, 16-17, 25-26, 29-47, 51-54, 57-75, 77-88, 91-94, 96, 99-101, 106, 112, 115-118, 122, 124, 127-134, 138, 148, 161-164, 171, 177-182

P

Paper form copyright registration, 25, 155
Parody, as fair use, 106, 109-110
Partnership, 177-179, 181
Patent, 18, 20, 27, 42, 48, 53-54
Peer-to-peer sharing, 17, 127
Penalty of perjury, under, 39, 47, 131-132
Perform, exclusive right to, 57-58, 62-63
Phonorecord, 28, 30-32, 59, 67, 72, 93, 154
Photographs, 15, 20, 46, 49, 115, 119, 123, 150, 156-158, 172-175
Pictorial, graphic and sculptural works, 26, 156
Plagiarism, 73
Poor man's copyright, 31-32
Prelinger Archives, 113-114
Preregistration, 160, 162, 168
Prima facie, registration as, 162
Privacy, right of, 18, 172-175; see also Right of Privacy
Profits, 10, 74, 75, 79-81, 84, 87-91, 94, 148, 179
Project Gutenberg, 19, 112-116
Proprietor, sole, 176, 181
Proving infringement, 78
Pseudonymous work, 42, 98-99
Public domain, 17, 19, 45, 51, 95, 97, 99-100, 112-116, 128, 141-142, 157, 164, 173, 182
Public domain work, 95, 100, 112-113, 173
Public performance, 28, 63, 128, 133-134
Public records, 43, 54, 169
Public.Resource.org, 19, 114
Publication, 18, 22, 27-29, 31, 33, 49, 51, 65, 79, 82, 86, 98-100, 105, 110, 116, 123, 141, 143, 148, 151, 156, 159-163, 168
Publicity, right of, 18, 124, 172-175; see also Right of Publicity
Published work, 28-31, 33, 35, 59, 82, 112, 153, 163

R

Recordation of transfers, 47, 101, 162
Registration of electronic copyright, step-by-step, 151
Remedies for infringement, 124; see also Infringement remedies
Reproduce or copy, exclusive right to, 51, 59, 71, 78
Research, pre-1978 online, 165, 168
Research, post-1978 online, 165
Restitution, 91, 93-94
Restored foreign copyrights, 142; see also General Agreement on Tariffs and Trade (GATT)
Right of Privacy, 18, 172-175
Right of Publicity, 18, 124, 172-175

S

Sale, of copyright; see Assignment
Sample filled-in forms, 17
Scènes à faire, 22, 36
Scholarship, as fair use, 108
Secretary of State, 44, 177, 181
Self-Research, step-by-step guide, 164-165
Service Mark, 49, 53-54, 180
Service Provider (SP), 52, 96, 127-134, 182
Service provider liability, 130
Shipping label, how to obtain, 158
Sole proprietorship, 18, 180
Sonny Bono Copyright Extension Term Act, 51
Soundtrack, motion picture, 30, 50, 154, 156
Special Purpose Entity or Vehicle (SPE or SPV), 177
Statute of limitations, civil infringement, 95
Statute of limitations, criminal infringement, 95
Statutory damages, 32-33, 74-75, 79-87, 140, 148, 162
Statutory license, 65, 67
Step-by-step guide, eCO electronic account, 147, 149
Step-by-step guide, electronic copyright registration, 17, 147, 149
Step-by-step guide, research USCO online records, 148
Storyboards, 15, 20, 41, 49, 96, 150, 156

T

Takedown notice, DMCA, 133, 182
Tangible medium of expression, 20-21, 23, 25, 40-41, 46, 86, 148, 150
Teaching, as fair use, 108; see also Education, as fair use
Trade Secret, 20, 27, 49, 53-54
Trademark, 18, 20, 27, 42, 49, 53-54, 64, 116, 174, 180
Transfers, 47, 101, 162; see also Recordation of transfers
Transfers, Motion pictures, 133
Transfers, termination of prior, 101
Transfers, VARA, 124
Transformative work, 46
Treaty, 15, 17, 29, 44, 51, 53, 97, 127-128, 134, 137-138, 140-144, 170
TRIPs, 53, 142-143

U

U.S. Code, Title 17, 50
U.S. Constitution, 48, 127
U.S. Copyright Office (USCO), 14, 17-18, 25-26, 35-36, 38, 43-44, 49, 71, 78, 128, 147, 149, 159, 163-164, 170
U.S. Customs Service, U.S. Customs & Border Protection, 93
U.S. Patent & Trademark Office (USPTO), 18, 27
Unauthorized use, 16-17, 49, 73, 75, 78-79, 95, 127, 174
Universal Copyright Convention, 143
Unpublished work, 28-31, 34-36, 44, 51, 82, 99, 106, 140, 144, 148, 150-151, 153, 160, 162-163
Unsolicited submission, 61
Uruguay Round Agreements Act (URAA), 53, 141-143
USCO, see U.S. Copyright Office (USCO)
USPTO; see U.S. Patent & Trademark Office (USPTO)

V

VARA, 17; see also Visual Artists Rights
  Act (VARA)
Visual art work; see Work of visual Art
Visual Artists Rights Act (VARA), 17, 21, 119, 121, 182
Visually perceptible copy, 31-32

W

Willful infringement, 81-83, 93
WIPO Copyright Treaty, 128, 142
Work of visual art, 120-122, 124
Work-made-for-hire, 37-42, 54, 59, 98-99, 119-123, 148, 151, 159, 180; see also Employment agreement
World Intellectual Property Organization (WIPO), 71, 92, 127, 142, 170
World Trade Organization (WTO), 143-144, 170
Writers Guild of America (WGA), 32, 89

CONTACT the PUBLISHER or the AUTHOR

Email: bizentinepress@gmail.com

ABOUT the AUTHOR

M. M. Le Blanc, JD, MBA, is an experienced international entertainment attorney and a veteran Hollywood film & television studio executive previously at Fox, Disney/ABC, Universal/Canal+, MGM/UA and more. Le Blanc has worked on hundreds of film and television productions, both as an executive and as an award-winning writer/producer. Le Blanc is also a multi-award-winning author of fiction and non-fiction whose numerous papers, articles and columns have been published in entertainment, law and business journals in the USA, Europe and Asia.

Le Blanc's academic experience includes positions as founding Academic Dean, Department Chair and Professor of intellectual property and entertainment law and business at film, law and business schools and universities in the United States and Europe.

Le Blanc is a frequent guest speaker and panelist at film festivals, pitchfests, film markets and entertainment industry conferences throughout the world. Le Blanc was selected one of the "Top Ten Young Working Women in America" and is a member of the Academy of Television Arts & Sciences (Television Academy) in Los Angeles.

www.ingramcontent.com/pod-product-compliance
Lightning Source LLC
Chambersburg PA
CBHW072007110526
44592CB00012B/1228